CW00855243

Bismillah
(In the Name of God)

Life Coaching for the Soul

JAVED KHAN

Copyright © 2017 Javed Khan.

All rights reserved. No part of this book may be reproduced, stored, or transmitted by any means—whether auditory, graphic, mechanical, or electronic—without written permission of the author, except in the case of brief excerpts used in critical articles and reviews. Unauthorized reproduction of any part of this work is illegal and is punishable by law.

ISBN: 978-1-4834-6762-7 (sc)
ISBN: 978-1-4834-6764-1 (hc)
ISBN: 978-1-4834-6763-4 (e)

Library of Congress Control Number: 2017904859

Because of the dynamic nature of the Internet, any web addresses or links contained in this book may have changed since publication and may no longer be valid. The views expressed in this work are solely those of the author and do not necessarily reflect the views of the publisher, and the publisher hereby disclaims any responsibility for them.

Any people depicted in stock imagery provided by Thinkstock are models, and such images are being used for illustrative purposes only. Certain stock imagery © Thinkstock.

Lulu Publishing Services rev. date: 3/30/2017

Contents

The Introduction

As a person who for many years has been trying to find his true Calling in life, through mostly torrid times for the most part I struck lucky when I met my friend Filipo.

His words have kept me sane through the darkest days of my life and have inspired me.

His words have comforted myself and have had a resounding positive effect on my life.

His words have inspired me to pull myself out of the depths of depressive behaviour and start to appreciate myself.

I consider it a Great Gift from GOD Almighty that I have had such an inspirational figure in my Life. I love him like a Brother and I cannot begin to thank him for all that he has done for myself and offcourse my children.

This book is Dedicated to my friend Filipo who like I said is a very Humble,Modest,Generous Man so It might surprise him to know that his brother thinks so highly of him.

His inspiration helped me keep on track with All the BISMILLAH PROJECTS which are being put in to motion and We intend for BISMILLAH to be a World Healing and Community Services Brand IN 5 YEARS.

His life coaching skills are to be admired and I am trying to persuade him to write on a multitude of subjects but he is too modest to even consider it, although I being myself will not give up.

We needed him as much as he needed us as BISMILLAH as an organisation is growing so will he grow with it .

I feel that with Filipo as a friend and adviser along with the passion that we all have for BISMILLAH as a Work in Progress We have a better than average Chance of Making a great success of Anything We are involved with Now or in the Future.

May GOD Almighty Guide, love and Bless Each Step we take.

Chapter One

The Power of Faith and Happiness

This book is about unreasonable Faith, Happiness and for You to live a fulfilled life without any guilt, whoever you are and wherever You are.

The purpose of this book is for you to become happier -to feel more of your good feeling and be more comfortable with the bad ones.

After doing the exercises and taking part in the self-hypno, Affirmations, Prayer, Meditation, God-Realization Exercises, Negative Fasting, Soul-Healing, Positive visualisation/meditation you will feel 100% better about the prospects for your Soul to find it's True Destiny(Eternal Peace and Happiness).

We as creative beings need time to enjoy what we take for granted and not fuss too much about the things we have no control over which are about 80%.

Over the next few hours or days or weeks or however long you take to read the book you will learn that you are far more in control of your own well being than you ever thought possible.

You will learn to make small changes in the way you feel, think or act and you will come to realize that these small changes can make a huge difference to the power of your soul-based Faith in the eventual outcome.

Throughout the book I will be using words and language patterns that will stimulate an emotional Reaction.

That's not to say that if you are angry, stressed out, anxious or depressed you can or should just pull yourself together.

Life is often difficult and blaming yourself for feeling bad is like trying to teach a dog to sing-it rarely works and it tends to annoy the dog.

How this will work

I have been a life coach for 10 years and have studied Islamic NLP, Hypnotherapy, Soul-healing and life coaching.

Over the time I have worked with a Variety of Clients.Some have been wealthy and some just getting by on a tight budget.

I have helped most of them to become happier and live more Soul fulfilling lives.

The reason I can work effectively with a TV star, a scientist and a housewife all in the same day is that I know something about each one of them which is also true of you:

YOU ALREADY HAVE EVERYTHING YOU NEED INSIDE YOU TO FEEL HAPPY AND LIVE A MEANINGFUL LIFE-THE ONLY QUESTION IS ACCESS.

<u>The choice to feel Happy</u>

No matter how many times I talk to people about the benefits of feeling happy to individual clients or groups, the initial responses are the same, they go some like these:

Is it not bad to feel happy when there is so much suffering in the world?

I would not want to feel happy all the time.

You cannot make me feel happy, you do not know my life or the things I have to deal with.

Finding excuses to be sad, angry or unhappy does not make you a bad person but it makes life hell for the poor things sharing the hole that you call life.

Excuses to feel happy are as follows:

It feels good.

It makes you healthier.

It makes you younger.

It makes you smarter.

It makes you more successful.

I will go in more detail in to all the above excuses just a little later, for now I have given you some things to think about or you can do the exercise of swapping excuses over.

When you are happy, nothing changes-but everything is different.

Mental mountains are reduced to molehills.

Problems that seemed hard and insoluble begin to dissolve in the light of your HAPPY AWARENESS.

Happiness is the process of creating thereby experiencing good feelings in your body and mind, moment by moment while pursuing your daily grind with life, it does not go away because your upset about doing it, it still needs to done.

<u>Happy realization</u>

1. As soon as you realize that happiness is a process,NOT a thing a miracle happens YOU ARE IN CHARGE.

2. You can do it, or not do it

3. You can get better at it.

You can master it and control it.

<u>The Myths about Happiness</u>

1. *I will be happy when ....Reach my goals, find love, get promotion, get new car or buy a new house.*

   Looking through the newspapers you can daily find a scandal concerning the rich and famous, proof that wealth alone does not make you happy.

2. *It is not right to be happy in certain situation.*

   Funerals, bad football matches and disappointments.

Just as the regular presence of fire engines at the scene of a fire does not mean that fire engines cause fire, the regular presence of unhappiness in certain situations does not mean that the situation caused the unhappiness.

The truth a little obvious:

while it may or may not be possible to be happy all the time,

It is certainly possible to be happy at any time.

A point of fact :

For every situation above where you think of as making you unhappy is simply an area where you think it is not appropriate to feel happy(funeral), or that feeling happy would be bad for you.

3. Unhappiness is good for us.

    The flip side of this is : *Whatever you can do with unhappiness you can do better when you are happy.*

    As long as we justify our unhappiness as being necessary or important, we will make sure we have more of it.

    We will find excuses for it and because it has been so much part of our lives we will at times do anything to have it, even some people suffering withdrawel symptoms.

    We all know some one in our past or present who use to want an argument or who love to see people fallout with each other, even stirring the pot to fuel the argument.

    <u>The comfort zone that some people crave is not always comfortable or ideal for happiness.</u>

Like with everything else you become what you practise.

1.   Think really hard about things that make you sad/Happy.

2.   Talk about those things in a sad voice/Happy voice with enthusiasm.

3.   Purse your lips(you can cry if you want)Hunch your shoulder and lower your eyes/smile or laugh with shoulders back, chest out with eyes bright.

These all work and we carry out all these action without thinking about them, because like all things we become what we practise.

The stories we tell ourselves about our lives have mostly nothing to do with what is really going on.

Our subconscious mind is constantly telling the story of our lives, minute by minute, second by second.

The power of Happiness and your God given right to be happy

My personal prayer (performed 5 times daily) or as a Famous life coach calls them POWER NAPS, he compares them to PITSTOPS on our Worldly/daily routines, challenges or up and downs.

Another famous author and playwright calls them Islamic Yoga for the Soul, because of the different positions of your body to recite your prayer.

•   In the name of GOD the most gracious, most merciful.

•   oh my lord i seek thy protection from the evil of the satan(in All his Guises) and his whispers in to the hearts of mankind.

•   oh my lord my intention is to perform this prayer

- You are glorified oh my lord, blessed is your name, Elevated is your majesty.

- There is no GOD but THEE.

- All praise and glory to ALLAH lord of the Worlds, Master of the day of Judgement, you alone I worship.

- Show me, My Lord and all of creation the Right Path.

- The Path of the GOD-conscious and the Good people of the present and the past.

not the path of those who cause pain, misery and disunity amongst Mankind.

God's PURPOSE flows to you without effort. it is the ULTIMATE GIFT. IT is given to you wherever you are and who ever you are, whatever label the world has given to you.

Politics has become nothing more than buying votes instead of living by true moral values.

What indeed has become of the Noble people who would strive for their right to live by the true and honest principles of open and honest faith in the promise of God, that the unjust will surely spend their real time in eternity in endless regret.

Do you not believe? Just think for a moment. Is it really worth it? Could you not be at least a little deceived by the illusory and ever-shifting life of this insane mortal world?

Do you really so disrespect the wisdom of the Saints, Sages and Prophets of all time?

YOU ARE A UNIQUE ENTITY AMONGST ALL OF CREATION

Are you really willing to sell your soul for a paltry handful of dirt?Faith is no accident - it can be perfected through self-education, direction, and healing. Your Faith is what you believe. And as you believe, so it shall be.

It is your Faith that controls your destiny. If your Faith is in alignment with A Benevolent Reality, your benevolent outcome is certain. So be certain that what you believe is true.

Perfect your Faith through constant Self Education. Feel yourself increasing in your Knowledge of God. We get what we expect.

Because I KNOW God is Good, I see and receive only Good. In order to receive good, don't focus on the good you wish to receive, focus on the knowing that God IS Good; on the Knowing of God.

This can be learned. And from this, all and only Good will come to you. Take your mind off what you want, for that is already known by God. Focus your mind on the Knowing of God and receive instant illumination.

The primary distortion to be overcome is that of a GOD who has no time to listen to my problems and why would HE CARE?You may be sceptical as you like, and then suddenly you are in tune with nature.

You start to live your life for the good of the world instead of being a selfish clod who moans constantly that the world will not devote all it's time to help you fix your life, which is never ending.

Start your day with" BISMILLAH(IN THE NAME OF GOD)" and you will be released of the extra Burden of ignorance and Disrespect which we as virtual nothing in the scheme of creation show regularly towards GOD ALMIGHTY,MASTER,CREATOR EXTRA-ORDINARY WHO HAS BREATHED HIS BEAUTIFUL SPIRIT IN TO EVERY SOUL.

THE CREATION OF LOVE

The creation of Love as the one thing that is the most powerful Force in creation is not up for question, neither is the power of Words described as the most powerful drugs known to mankind.

Although it is what is described as a ANOMALY, a thing described as an object but does not have form, just like Happiness, misery, anger, evil or hate.

It would be interesting if the above were objects that you could buy, probably cheaper on the internet, if you chose.

There is but One Reality, and that Reality is infinite and unconditional Conscious Benevolence, manifesting itself as a Divine Source of endless and eternal Love, Care and Resource, unlimited Generosity and Provision from unseen and unknown sources.

This is no fleeting thought. This is an ever-present reality. It is not to be held in the mind alone but through the process of realization, incorporated into your being with an ever-increasing depth of perception and awareness, that through this actual embodiment, ever-more increasing benefit may be derived.

It is a classic mistake on the part of many theologians to emphasize service as a means to the 'reward' of realization, but true service is a being resurrected as the product of realization and often, no matter how selfless or devout, service can fail as a means.

This is because it is imperative to realize that realization need only be realized, otherwise the fact that it is present already and always has been might be denied, and it cannot be had if its eternal presence is not recognized. Contemplate One Reality- Not Two!

Hold before your mind's eye only the perfect image that Universal Mind has of your body.

"There is one rule that will help anyone keep healthy. That rule is to forget your nerves and your bottles, and hold before your mind's eye only the perfect image that Universal Mind has of your body.

That is the surest way to keep free from sickness. Know that Universal Mind never created disease, which is but an illusion of your conscious mind.

Know that mind is the only creator that as one famous scholar puts it, "There is nothing, either good or bad, but thinking makes it so." Know that you have the say as to what that thinking shall be. Know, therefore, that by holding a perfect image of your body in your thoughts you can make your body perfect

DISCOVERING THE MIRACLE

"Praise and Gratitude to Allah Who has guided us to 'This'. And we could not be among the guided (to 'This') were it not for the guidance of Allah." ~The Qur'an

"...and how can I explain to you what 'This' is?"

One thought of 'Absence" leads to the world of error. One true thought that there is no absence of life, substance and intelligence in my idea of good, restores to us our rightfully divine inheritance.

Chapter Two

What Are the Powers of Bismillah

The Miracle is, by definition, Divine. We All need The Miracle in our lives. We either recognize our lives as The Miracle we need or we do not. But in either case, we need The Miracle in our lives.

Many people have health who are not necessarily healed. People who are healed are no longer concerned with health and that is why it is granted to them.

Their very disconcern for it is why it is granted them. What is it that healed people are concerned with? They are concerned with The Miracle. They are literally fascinated by it; in awe of it. It occupies their every thought and glance and moment.

"One Perfect Thought of God, inserted into the body, will heal you perfectly!"

What a profound thought! Can we even begin to fathom the reality of that? Why, Yes! We can if we want to. If we are interested in truth in any fashion, we must be fascinated by the potential offered in this one idea. For he who can accept his true Identity is truly saved.

And his salvation is the gift he gives to everyone, in gratitude to Him

Who pointed out the way to happiness that changed his whole perspective of the world."

All your images of winter I see against your sky.

I understand the wounds that have not healed in you.

They exist because God and Love have yet to become real enough to allow you to forgive the dream.

The moment your reach outside of yourself you have forgotten yourself!

It is only in the state of higher consciousness and God consciousness that an individual can move out of conflicts of ego personality and experience inner balance, harmony and peace.

Unhappy people have false beliefs!

The True Way is a Mercy to the Worlds and a Healing for the Hearts of Men, women, children and All of Creation.

Please note that the consequences of ignorance can be devastating. Just look around you.

Different religions, different countries and different people oblivious to the Unity of All.

Are the people of war the same as the people of peace? Are they even living in the same reality?

The Thinking after Surrender is different from the thinking before.

ABIDANCE - WHAT EVERYONE WANTS TO KNOW

You dwell not here but in Eternity. You travel but in dreams, while safe at home.

Abidance in Arabic is Baqa`. Baqa` means permanence, establishment, permanence of abode, established, an established reality, a foundation, a fundamental base of operations, security, permanence and reality, a place from which to manifest love.

It cannot be found in the worldly life and cannot be found by seeking, yet most people seek it in a worldly existence which is only a reflection of the truth of their quest.

Only a similitude of permanence can be established in this world because everything in life is consistently changing on all levels at all different velocities or rates of speed.

Permanence can be recognized only in the spiritual world, and this simply because it is our Reality.

When that permanence is determined, established and recognized to be the only real permanence, all purpose will shift and actions will come from that place only. They will then reflect the feeling of truth and reality that others seek, and success of outward accomplishment will ensue.

Baqa`, or permanence, is a gift from Allah! We already have it! We need only to abide in it. And to do this we need only to maintain our conscious awareness of God, our God-Consciousness, and this means not allowing ourselves to fall back into the dream.

Allah is permanent, and this is without question, so is the manifestation of His creation that is beyond the time and space of worldly existence.

we are that manifestation.

By that I do not mean us as the temporary and transitory manifestation of this life, which is only a moment in which we may discover ourselves and choose to abide in the truth or ignore it and pursue the illusion.

It is not that this temporary and transitory life is meaningless but that it is only a tool, a moment in eternity, by which we may gain knowledge of our transcendent nature.

It is by means of this life that we gain our true recognition of God. It is by the very means of this life that we may learn to transcend it and know of and abide in our life forever in a garden not of our own making.

That is why I say often that the purpose of life, death, and everything in between is Self- and God-realization.

Once that transcendence is determined and established (baqa`), and that is the goal of all genuine effort, the life in this world becomes easy and is a gift, a trivial and insignificant, nevertheless substantial and respectable, indication of our Real life.

So seek, O seekers of God, your real life with Allah, and then let all "else", if there is an "else", be added unto you. For with this peace you have all peace, and without it you have no real peace at all.

It is on this foundation of truth and permanence that a life of religion and spirituality can be built.

ENLIGHTENMENT AND THE TRUE PATH

My writing is for the mind interested in the parallels between Islamic Psychology and Healing and Western Psychology and Healing, attempting to clarify the Healing Relationship between Psychology, Spirituality and Physical Health.

Islamic Psychology is about understanding the Spiritual Roots of True Faith, the Real Islam, as practiced by the loving majority, and the Healing power of Original Islamic Faith, which is the body of teachings for the aspirants of True Loyal Faithfull behavior towards all creation for the Love of the one true CREATOR,GOD ALMIGHTY, given different names by different people over time .

FINDING YOUR AUTHENTIC SELF

THE DEMANDING SELF

Demanding that the world be the way it needs and wants it to be and denying that healing is possible or necessary - demanding outward change with threats and violence, while refusing inward change on religious grounds,

THE SELF-REPROACHING SELF

The self-reproaching self, who studies religion for its true purpose and as it is meant to be studied, for self-correction, purification and proximity to God - not for world control through the use of force, punishment and shame/guilt tactics.

THE INSPIRED SELF

The inspired, believing self, knowing that religion and spirituality is the healing and the means to the real success.

Enlightenment is attainment (Self-realization) based upon understanding the relationship between Divinity, Psychology, True Surrender and Physical Health. It is the goal and the "work" of many paths.

Experience and in-depth study and understanding of the significance of religion in general and the teachings of Islam in particular. Furthering this understanding becomes the interest and ongoing work of the enlightened few, for a deeper knowledge of the nature of Unity.

THE NATURE OF UNITY

The emphasis on Surrender and the healing of the body of it's physical and emotional separation from the oneness of reality and begins the real process of learning and teaching - from "Islam" (Surrender) to "Iman" True Knowledge based Faith.

In many schools these distinctions are not made, as, being only distinctions, they are not considered relevant. They may, however, be of use in relating to the Original Islamic path .

Self-Realization is the basic qualification for any spiritual teacher,Being the goal of every True Believer.

It is only from it that one can bring others to it, and one's ability to stay in it will match and facilitate one's ability to deal with the difficulties of one's students in attaining it.

This then becomes the "new work" - staying IN the Energy - Abidance - and offering the same opportunity to others. And what is "The Energy"? Enlightened Living - Living in the Light of Love and Peace from God.

Many conquest of colonies over the centuries have started with the oppressors playing DIVIDE AND RULE, which roughly meant that the invaders did not have to use so much military might, they used the Ego of the inhabitants against them .

In my opinion Evil in all it's different forms has played Divide and Rule with the human race.

God Almighty has been put to one side for the sake of vanity, ego, materialism and ignorance.

History has even been altered for the masses to be subjugated with guilt,Emotional blackmail and a slow destruction of the Soul.

Shame on the Shepherds for mistreating the sheep.

INDIVIDUAL REALIZATION

As each of us comes to realization, we realize that our individual manifestation of our realization counts.

If not just because of the value of expression to each of us personally, but because we will be led to discover that the discoveries we are being led to discover are truly discoveries, and as such are significant contributions to human evolution and education. Hence we each teach from our experience.

The "mysteries" of life are unknown, until they are investigated.

The primary obligation

This has always seemed of utmost practicality to me, because I somehow understood that if I did not complete my primary obligation to know God, I would always be remiss in that. And the nagging therefrom of my conscience would distract me from my wholehearted attention to anything "else", anyway.

Even more attractive than that was the claim that All could indeed, in the reality of one life time, be known.

That's way more than a neurotic under-achiever with a huge compensatory ego-need could ever resist, and the fact that it meant selling my life down the river of chance was small potatoes for such a large payoff.

DIRECT LINK TO GOD,YOU DO NOT NEED A MIDDLEMAN

GOD Almighty wants to hear from you, your Real self,Are you shy, embarrased to speak to Him or do you need someone else to ask for you?In Original Islam you do not need a middleman(Priest,Mullah or Rabbi,Guru or Mentor) You have a DIRECT line to GOD,Call Him any time, any place or anywhere.

What's more, as I studied the claim more carefully, I came to understand that in spite of the fact that I could enter the path for all the "wrong" ego reasons, i.e. to get back, to say I told you so, to "prove" superiority and that I was right, it was, nevertheless, the right thing to do, because in reality, we are releasing our need to be driven to our need to understand, and, in doing so, fulfilling the requirements of our ultimate destiny and our primary purpose in life and on earth.

That is to know God as He wishes us to know Him.

The beauty of this is that in knowing God and because of the nature of the way He has created us, we get to know ourselves also, and thereby attain to the keys to a deep knowing of humanity and thereby to all knowledge.

It is obviously not to say that one human brain could contain all the knowledge available to humanity.

No, that's not what I mean.

What I mean is thatThere is a key to understanding all that we need to understand in any given moment.

The cost of that key is the sacrifice of our presumptions.

THE POWER OF INTUITION (Emotionally in tune with yourself)

It might be called total all out commitment to intuition in such a way that intuition is all there is and there is nothing left to judge it or to call it intuition.

When we're living in intuition there is only the reality from which it comes. There is no longer the comparative judging mindset that refers to intuition as something "other".

By the same token there is no longer the mindset that refers to soul as something "other", or to God as something "other". There is simply the reality of one's individual life, unfolding itself according to Divine plan, free of the influence of preferences.

In the "realized, or "enlightened" mind, the distinction is clear between the "reality" of one's individual life and the "illusion" of one's individual life.

While that distinction may not be clear to people still caught up in the illusion, it is certainly very clear to the people who have done the work necessary to see through the illusion.

It is these people who by virtue of their ability to distinguish the truth and reality in themselves, are able to help others to distinguish it in themselves.

This is the distinction above all other distinctions. <u>This is the Philosopher's stone, the red Sulfur and the Midas touch, by which</u> lead is transformed into gold.

<u>Freedom from illusion is the ultimate freedom. Knowledge of truth is the ultimate knowledge.</u>

AN INTIMATE RELATIONSHIP

It is that the fulfillment of your primary obligation to know God intimately is your primary obligation, and that after that, the ease of life and livelihood would appear in genuine form, not just another temporary respite. This is the "Authentic Self" . It is the basis of peaceful co-existence and the foundation of lasting civilization.

It is that once you make the fulfillment of your primary obligation your primary obligation, it becomes easier and long distances are traversed quickly.

Making it your primary obligation is your primary obligation. Now see how simple that is, but you will find that it is easy, except to the Mentally enslaved from all sides(including gnostics and agnostics).

Shame on the shepherds for misguiding the sheep, letting them wander in to danger.

Shame on the shepherds for making the sheep helpless by keeping them ignorant of the truth and the dangers.

THE KEY TO THE SECRET

There is only one secret, and that is your secret. When your secret is unlocked by the company of a TRUTH SEEKER, you too, become your own master. The essence of the religion of Islam is to unlock the secret in all of humanity, making each and every one of us a master and a gnostic and a knower of the secret.

The secret can be and has been formulated, and there are three levels of knowing and practicing this formula.

The first level is on the tongue, holding it there, treasuring it there and valuing it there. These are the people of knowing the truth and they are in two categories.

There are those desiring to know more of the truth and those thinking that their knowledge of the truth is as far as it goes and that there is no more than that.

If they treasure it as a key to deeper understanding and further search and walking in the way of God, then they will be led by their desire to know, and caused by their destiny to encounter a trail that will lead them further than they could have ever imagined. These are the travelers on the way.

If however they value their knowledge in the way of knowing that it provides for them the medicine for their personal insecurities in the form of the illusion, dream and goal of material acquisition and stability, then they will be hesitant if not completely resistant and vehemently against the idea of learning more. They will stop with the outside picture and claim loudly and vociferously that there is no more to life and religion than what they understand of it, and claim majority agreement as proof.

The second level of knowledge is that of the sincere students who treasure the knowledge as it should be treasured and use it to guide them though the adventurous waters of life, trusting in its source, and thereby knowing that it comes from and will lead them to the solid shores on the "other" side.

The third level of knowing is held by the masters of surrender, who honor the inner tradition to its utmost, and thereby attain to the knowing without knowing, that the knowing, the knower and the known are all one and the same. There is no "other". There is only the travel from illusion to truth, from fanciful imaginings to an imperishable reality.

It is not beyond the power of God to create in such a way that the essence of the secret of His creation can be delivered in a simple formula. After all, The Old Testament states that in the beginning there was a word.

The first could be the Divine Name of God - Al-llah! His manifestation of Self Knowledge and the means by which He is known. The second could be simply the word "BE!" For it is said that with this word He brought all of creation into being.

The third, and the "formula" that I wish to introduce here, is what is known in Islam as being the "Kalima Tayyiba" or the Best of Words, "La ilaha illa `llah, Muhammadun Rasulullah", sometimes and loosely translated as "There is no God but One (Al-llah!) and Muhammad is the Prophet."

The point here is not to argue what the "word" might be by which all creation came into existence. It is only to exemplify that it is possible for the Divine Creator to bring creation into being in such a way as to make it easy for us to know Him, and His "secrets", including His guidelines for correct, constructive and successful behavior.

That it is possible to make that information known in the shortest amount of time to the largest number of people.

THE SECRET FORMULA

This formula is the holiest affirmation and the divine words of truth to the believers, and it is not contradictory in spirit to the truth in any other religion, psychology or spiritual realization path.

This formula leads from and to the truth of the Author of the whole of creation itself. It is the guiding light of Original Religion and the basis of the realization that can bring from us moments of inspiration that can guide worlds and nations.

Bearing witness to the truth of these words - that there is only One God, and that this testimony is and was the message of the Prophet Muhammad - is such a personally revealing and heart opening experience, that it is repeated with love, devotion and gratitude more than five times daily.

This witnessing is enshrined in holy mosques, hearts, ritual purification, prayer and worship all over the world by an ever-increasing number of people coming to this belief.

Only 20% of the Islamic world actually have Arabic as their first language, the other 80% follow Islam, reading their prayers without fully understanding what they are saying when they pray to GOD ALMIGHTY.

I believe this has to change with FULL EMPHASIS given to understanding and reciting the prayer in the persons own Language, for example English.

I have been reading my prayers like the vast majority of muslims of non-arab background in Arabic for years, which I was never encouraged to Question.

Bewildering, as I cannot speak or understand arabic, so I learnt the meaning of the whole daily prayers in English.

To Empower the Everyman and to encourage more knowledge among the masses.

All real faith should be Directed to the Author of Creation No Agent or middleman Needed or required.

PRAY IN A LANGUAGE YOU ARE THINKING

NOT IN A LANGUAGE THAT YOU ARE NOT THINKING IN ALL THE FOUNDING FAITHS WERE SENT AS A GUIDE IN A CHOSEN LANGUAGE OF THE PEOPLE OF THE TIME FOR AN AWAKENING OF THE SOUL LINKED TO GOD ALMIGHTY,WITH LANGUAGE AS NO BARRIER.

ORIGINAL FAITH IS A DIRECT LINK TO GOD ALMIGHTY,NO MIDDLEMAN OR AGENT NEEDED.

LOOK AT HISTORY.

LEARN AND AWAKEN.

I now read the 5 daily prayers in English,The difference is Astounding.

Once one has reached to the conclusion that these words were designed to bring one to, one knows all that one needs to know.

In that knowing, all masters are peers, and it no longer matters by which tradition that knowing came to be.

This knowing, although with great sacrifice attained, is, by its new availability, made that much closer to the reality of the deep understanding of the "common" person.

It is not only closer in reach to the students who know about it and want it, or are searching for it and will find it. The charismatic force of yet another enlightenment, a lifting of the burden of not quite knowing for sure, of another realized being, reaches out into the fabric of society stabilizing and encouraging ordinary people to be satisfied and grateful for their lives.

It is yet another spiritual vote encouraging gratitude, peace and trust in the plan of the Divine.

So there it is. Want to know the way and the light? Understand the truth of these words. Walk in the path of those who are on IT.

THE ARRIVAL OF THE SOUL

A NEW PERSPECTIVE ON THE ORIGIN AND HEALING OF DEPRESSION

Can you understand how, in early infancy, initial perception of the outside world causes a brief and barely noticeable sense of loss of connection with source?

Ever noticed how a child will immediately retreat to the safety of the familiar upon first contact with something outside itself, something "strange"?

This "retreat" is in response to the sense of lost connection felt upon initial contact with something "other". It is not, as commonly thought, a 'reaction' to the other, but a response to the felt sense of lost connection. Understand?

The point of this observation is to illumine the inability of the immature being to focus upon outward object relativity while remaining in secure connection with the inward reality. It is because of this immaturity that life is considered to be a process of "either/or".

The idea of "both" is nowhere in sight - it is inconceivable or considered impossible.

This is the origin of that deep feeling or fear that we all have had (and ignore) that somehow we are selling our souls, and for a paltry price, specifically, for a "life" in this world.

It is this inability that the life experience is created to correct. It's not that we're born imperfect, but that we're born to learn. How to enjoy a heavenly life and still remain in gratitude.

How to live life to its fullest.

Undaunted, however, and due to the overwhelming, yet gently initiatory and loving, ongoing growth of the infant, the world as such continues to introduce itself.

The sense of lost connection becomes more commonplace, ordinary and acceptable, eventually disappearing altogether.

Continuing his exploration, the youth eventually shifts his/her focus completely from identification with the inward connection to identification with outward objects.

He develops his sense of being able to "relate" to his environment, in whatever form it may appear. His focus shifts from being inwardly connective to outwardly 'relative'. His manner of "relating" becomes his personality, and he begins to believe that this is who he "really" is.

Little does the infant know that with this inevitable shift of focus the seed is sown for his journey through life, only to discover that there is no end to it, and that the world cannot be, like the toys of his childhood, 'had'.

His perceptions will return, overwhelmed and defeated.

When he sees the futility and emptiness of endless desire, he will begin to remember, miss and wish for the comfort of that sense of connection, only to find that it is lost.

He then discovers the taste of hopelessness, feels trapped, and becomes depressed.

Few there are who can then reconnect with their source completely on their own. So into the 'adult' world messengers, messages and teachers are sent to assist in the process of establishing the true inward connection in the beings of those who seek it and those who are truly ready for it.

When the connection is established, a genuine compassion and understanding emerges, and the being desires to manifest and so offers a helping hand.

Such is the natural emergence of the "teacher" within us all. Few are they who accept the offer, but eventually a small but growing community is established for the purposes of self-exploration and devising new ways to teach this lost knowledge.

The Religion of Islam (Surrender) was sent for exactly that purpose - to reunite humanity and show the way back to Source - revealing a universally applicable method for personal and social evolution.

Religion is not enough. This 'evolution', or maturation, requires the desire and will of the individuals. It is called willingness, and it is this factor that determines, by its presence or its absence, who will choose to evolve, or not, at that moment.

So it is that even within the religion of Islam, with all of its signs and encouragement, few there are who choose to investigate these signs and add their energy to the perpetuation of the revealed science of evolution.

The followers of truth in this world who study and practice this science Honestly and with Loyalty for sake of the whole of creation.

Their souls are bare. You stand present and unashamed, basking in the Mercy and Benevolence of the God who made you, reaching out with affirmations of your love for All Allah's Creations in nature, knowledge and love, inviting others to be free of the chains that burden them.

To free themselves from their emotional bonds and attachments to their desires, which only distract them and detract from their innate deep knowing, trust and ultimate success.

A Solid & Confirmed INNER CONNECTION is the Key to Every Success!

In Arabic this knowledge is called soul purification; those who study it and learn it are called True Muslims. And according to the masters of this study, the religion of Islam (Surrender) was sent for exactly that purpose - to reunite humanity and show the way back to Source - revealing a universally applicable method for personal and social evolution.

Chapter Three

Bismillah and Creation

THE TRUTH AND TRUTH OF ORIGINAL FAITH

So original Religion can be thought of as the psychology of Islam (Surrender), and Islam is considered by the all the hierarchy of all World religions to be the revealed science of evolution and transformation, or soul purification,Whether they formerly Acknowledge this FACT or keep it hidden from their FLOCKS.

Islam (Surrender) is the ORIGINAL FAITH that All the messengers of GOD brought as a Gift to their Respective Nations ever since Time Began.

The true path to find the Real purpose of the Soul.

A Solid & Confirmed INNER CONNECTION is the Key to Every Success!

TOWARDS A UNIVERSAL PSYCHOTHERAPY

World Peace and soul Psychology - East and West

"Remember Me, and I will remember you" (The Qur`an)

On the Notable Absence of Islamic Psychotherapy in a Crazy World.

Heaven on earth is the quest of every human being.

As a westerner growing up in a war-torn world but nevertheless self-centered enough to not get involved with anything that might threaten my pursuit of religious and spiritual knowledge.

I have always wondered at the lack of a universally dominant healing philosophy by which all grievances are addressed, and all people happy, thriving and cooperative. This is clearly not the case, but why not?

Is it possible that there might be a universal truth by which all people will live as equals in a happy, thriving world?

Does this need to be in the "afterlife"? Can we not have it now? The quest for the reality of this question is a form of spiritual selfishness that is so inherent within us that it cannot be reversed or destroyed.

This "heaven on earth" is the quest of every human being. It manifests in everything done. We have simply made an end of the means and forgotten our true goal.

The exotericists of religion tell me that this heaven is not for this world, but in an afterlife for people who do "good" in this life.

That leaves me with the need to clarify the meaning of "good".

What is the "good" that I want to do in order to be accepted into the heaven that is in the "afterlife"? And does that heaven exist now ? Can I, by virtue of some deed or deeds, live in that heaven now?

It's obvious that children are heavenly, and that more and more of them are coming into the world. It's obvious that there is enough deep, heavenly peace in the world to go around to everyone.

Are not sleeping children (at least, temporarily) in heaven? Why then are we in such a turmoil?

Understanding the Doctrine of Original Sin-

The basis of the problem

All Muslims claim their book to be the very healing that the world needs but most prefer others to understand it and explain it to them before they themselves will do it.

An active minority lays claim to their understanding of the meaning and significance of the book through the auspices of state sponsored teachers who rely on the simple fundamentals of religion in order to teach.

A closer investigation reveals a startling, even deliberate similarity in teaching methodology to simple Christianity. The theory being that it seems to work for them, so why shouldn't it work for us? But these simple fundamentals are predicated upon an intensely Roman Catholic premise, that of Original Sin.

The basic premise and motivational factor of the fundamentalists (in any religion) is to state that we (people) are bad, evil (or at least stupid) and surely destined for hell if we do not follow and support them and believe as they believe.

Scratch the skin of any fundamentalist(Muslim, Christian, Jew, Anarchist, Hindu or any other) and you will find an unremitted terror.

As long as Religion is being "preached" this way, i.e. without the fears of the people being addressed, the road to "salvation" will always be through the fires of war.

Hence the origins of unwarranted militancy resulting in the actions of suicide and terrorism(whether it's state sponsored or individual,East or west, in different Guises, afterall Evil can disguise itself, only to reveal itself when the soul is DAMNED FOR EVER)

We do not know God as God deserves to be known. Because we do not trust in God as God deserves to be trusted(Hence the need for agents or middlemen). If we haven't tasted the true trust in God then we owe it to ourselves at least once in life. We've tasted everything else, why not the trust of ALLAH?

Fear is not the right way to teach anything, let alone religion and especially Islam.

These disturbed "teachers" dismiss the meaning of the truthful Islamic traditions that support the existence of a basic inherent innocence both in themselves and in others. " Our religion is all courtesy", -' Surrender is the way of nature', "Children are born Muslims (i.e. in a state of Surrender)",

"Allah (God) did not create to punish", "Do not become the slaves of religion", .

If they do not throw them out they put such a twist upon them as to virtually nullify their original simple meaning.

We have changed the religions of truth over the centuries into lives of fearful denial "All else but me is wrong and bad, all this is bad and only good as I see it is good". Negating this and negating that. There is no affirmation except lip service to the active role of God in everything.

So my question is, what is the "good" that will guarantee my eternal life in heaven, and if I do it all in this life, will I be able to feel and live in that heaven even while still in this life as well?

If the answer to the second part of that question is yes, then that means that that heaven exists now, not later, and is merely on "another" but concurrent plane of existence. It also means that with the right amount and quality of effort, it can be perceived.

Well, if it can be perceived, then I want to go there right now and make it my permanent residence, so what is this effort, the right amount and quality of which will allow me to perceive it? And is not that particular effort the very "good" that I am seeking to do?

All religions say that surrender to God puts us in heaven. And Surrender to God right here and now is exactly the meaning of the word "Islam". So Surrender (Islam) puts us in the garden.

So that's the answer to my question, and that's what I want to do, Surrender.

Surrender to whom and surrender what? The first part seems easy, surrender to the existence of God, but how do I know who God is? And as for "what" do I surrender, I might start with my contentious ways. Letting go of my defenses and letting be what may.

That means that the garden is our natural state, the state of peace and surrender. So what state is it that takes us out of the garden and puts us in jeopardy (harm's way) of the fire? Why the state of anger, of course. It is fear and concern for self, not true self-knowing, that is the beginning of separation and mistrusting

THE DOCTRINE OF ORIGINAL SIN IN ISLAM

"But", you say, "Islam does not have any Doctrine of Original Sin".

And I say, "Exactly, so why are so many Muslims (The preponderant majority, I observe) behaving towards Islam exactly in the same manner as Christians behave toward their religion?"

I say it's because it is being, and has been, taught to them in exactly the same way.

what do I mean by that?

The Muslim societies have completely adopted the west as a standard - with its questioning, exploratory language, and it's scientific absolutism, and its ingrained religious values, which are unnoticeably inherent within the structure of the language itself.

Since for a most part English (not Arabic) is the second and many times primary language to most of them, and the idea of "meaning" means "what does it mean in English", or "how would your translates that into English", the question of meaning depends a lot upon whom you are asking.

The real meanings and goals of Islam are and can teach them from the inner heart experience in any language. These are the people who can set right the misunderstandings inherent in teaching Islam in a language colored by another religion or materialistic mindset.

Now we are back to the problem of practicing Islam in a Christian culture and language and cleansing ourselves of a fundamentalist Christian influence.

Cleansing Original religion of a fundamentalist Tag.

Cleansing ourselves of our Christian influence has a lot to do with understanding the root of the "Original Sin" theory and how it plays out psychologically in daily and religious life. That is why it is to awaken To

THE IMPORTANCE OF SELF-REALIZATION

Surrender is the means to Self-Realization. Self-Realization is a Functional Awareness of Soul, i.e. Soul-Recognition.

Soul-recognition is the source of health and healing. Soul is each individual's manifest portion of unlimited divine love.

It is maintained by the constant, unfathomable, unending outpouring of divine love that maintains creation and everything in it in perfect, beautiful, seamless harmony.

Self, the physical body, is the means by which we perceive Soul, and thereby receive divine love, hence the importance of cleaning it and keeping it pure, for God alone.

This purification implies the investigation and removal of the inner causes to not receive divine love that have been planted there by environmental inheritance.

Surrender means letting go of the fight, laying down the weapons of war, allowing God's will to unfold as it may, and relinquishment of preference or attachment to outcome.

It is most often done upon discovery of a teacher or a path. Enough surrender and your true self will finally emerge. Your true self, or soul, is the means by which your body receives love.

Your false self (ego) is the means by which it receives the punishment that it is due in your mind.

If you use your body for the accomplishment of artificial goals for the sake of artificial responsibilities, then in effect you are saying that is what this body is for, it is not worth anything else, and that's certainly a form of self-punishment.

People will lay their bodies on the line for their ideals, no matter how perverse those ideals may be. The last thing on their minds is the concept of laying down the struggle. They call it "giving up" and will "never" do it.

Peace is a requisite for health. A peaceful heart is the absolute requisite for a peaceful body.

Without peace there can be no perception of love and it is the perception of love that heals the body, heart and mind.

Where does this love come from? What is the means by which we can attain to it and perceive it and receive it? It is not outside of us, so we have to stop looking.

It's only when we stop seeking that we can feel.

As long as we are seeking we're still in our minds and projecting a time or a place when or where we will discover something.

That "something" is not "located" in any place or time. It is not "out there" somewhere to be "found". "The goal is not found by seeking, but only the seekers find it".

Soul does not need healing. That would be like saying God needs healing. God does not need healing. God is the healer.

It is from God that the energy of love, support and maintenance of the soul comes. So the Soul, created in God's image, and supported completely in its capacity as the highest and most perfect manifestation of God's Self-Recognition, Love and Perfection, does not need healing.

It has and is everything we need.

The self needs to discover the soul completely in order to rise to its fullest potential. It does this by means of dissolving itself in the remembrance of God.

As I'm sure you are aware, the Original Muslims HAD a fine tradition of perfecting the remembrance of God. The basics of the myriad techniques developed by them were revealed to us by God during the revelation of His most recent manifestation of what to believe and how to believe it, the religion of Islam (which by the way, means "The Way to Surrender"). Hence it is said in The Qur'an,

"Surely it is in the Remembrance of God that the Hearts find Satisfaction."

This singular phrase is the basis of all Islamic healing, realization and psychotherapeutic techniques, not to mention all of the other estimable social skills that arose as a result of those peaceful years in Islamic history.

It is also the ultimate outcome of Western spiritual psychology.

Soul-power is the single most constructive, beautifying and life-enhancing creative force in history, and conversely, ego and fear accomplish only destruction.

The entire Islamic civilization - the one from which the crusaders, thence the Knights Templar, thence the Masons, thence the modern Western world as we know it today learned the simple sciences of architecture, agriculture and irrigation, personal and public hygiene, just taxation and social equity, to mention only a few - was built upon this principle. How then can it not be personally important and socially significant now?

SPIRITUAL PSYCHOLOGY AND THE HUMAN SITUATION -

WHY ISLAM?

The entirety of this work is an in-depth exploration of spiritual psychology and the human situation, written as it occurs to me.

It seems to have become a complete explanation and reply to the question, "Why Islam?"

The end result of my entire exploration, I discover, is that the human situation without guidance and knowledge from the Divine is at best an expression of need and a genuine prayer for exactly such guidance.

In the midst of all that, I describe the true joy, enlightenment, wisdom and satisfaction found in true Surrender, which is the experiential meaning of "Islam".

It is from within our Surrender that we discover our prayer for guidance, and from within the revelation of Islam that we receive our prayer for guidance.

It is only self-satisfaction that claims no need for guidance. Both the wise and the weak know that guidance is necessary and pray for it.

So be wary of the satisfied self. It is only one step on the way and becomes a hindrance if one tarries there.

The human situation is one of need, but need of what we already have, Divine Grace. The problem is simply that we are so imperiled, threatened and intimidated by the life as we see it in the world view we've acquired that we ascribe a singular reality to our lives and problems and lose our focus on the Mercy and Grace from it's Author.

We become so embroiled in the problem as we see it that we cannot focus on the Solution, as God sees it. We even take our respective religions not for their own sake but for the sake of solving our problems, and that they may mercifully do.

We then find that we cannot stay in the resolution without coming to the aid of our religion. In other words, to learn and teach our own discoveries is the way to stay in them.

Intention and sincerity are shifting targets until they aren't any more. Our intentions for the study of religion and spirituality are rarely correct at first but nevertheless we can gain results according to them.

We would not think of coming to the aid of a path that has not proven itself to work for us. We rarely consider what that path might demand of us after it has worked for us.

If we were to know that in advance we might consider not entering into it at all, in spite of all the good we might gain from it.

Few of us like to pay back, but it seems that payback is what any good path demands in exchange for Abidance. After all, how can one stay in a way that has accepted and healed one except by taking up it's ways. And, after all, why wouldn't one want to?

DO NOT IGNORE GOD,DO NOT SHARE HIS ALMIGHTY POWER WITH ANOTHER OF HIS CREATION.

So sincerity demands that we must be always purifying our intentions.

We find that we must then, in order to stay in the "heaven" that God and good religion promises and delivers, become committed to the ways of that heaven.

Our commitment becomes our religion and our religion, whichever one keeps us there, becomes our commitment.

This is where most of us falter and fall back, but the Solution requires, from a healed and realized standpoint, the learning and teaching of the way which brings to us personally so much relief, joy and satisfaction.

ALL ORIGINAL RELIGION STARTS WITH A HARDWIRED BELIEF IN THE ONE TRUE ALMIGHTY GOD and that means All HUMAN PSYCHE, before contamination or confusions.

Mankind does not like simplicity in existence as can be seen by the slow suicide witnessed by GOD Almighty.

These teachings go to great length in explaining the healing of spiritual psychology and the particular predicament in which humanity finds itself.

They are in the broadest sense the teachings of Islam, but personalized and represented through the eyes of one who has walked through it, stays in it, and teaches from personal experience.

This work is an exposition of the true meaning and universal application of the three most commonly known and used Arabic words, Al-llah!, Islam and Muslim, and the three active principles supportive and causative of the Spiritual Revolution.

These three principles are: The Imperative of Spiritual Unity, The Universal Salvation Principle and The Psychology of Surrender. Together they are the real force of our esoteric guidance.

The activity of these principles is unstoppable, for they are the direct power of God's intervention for the benevolent destiny of Humanity.

These are the activities that we have all been praying for and to which the Surrendered are Surrendered. They are the Power Of We.

For it is when we lend our energy to God's purpose that changes begin to manifest.

The reality of these principles has always been in effect, but our conscious Surrender to them is catalyzing their acceleration, speeding their conclusion, and turning the world of conflicting religious beliefs into a world dominated by peace, love and co-operation.

The negative effect of activity not in harmony with the peaceful needs of the world has it's benefit also in that it has shown us what the alternative to world peace and harmony is.

The function of dysfunction is to increase intelligence. Let us say that our intelligence is rapidly increasing as old cells are dying and new ones are springing into an increasingly responsive and hospitable world.

It's understanding the undesireable alternative that forces us to realize that The Future is Peace (or there is no Future).

Upon comprehending the "Three Words -Three Principles", we will then easily see and understand the Confluence of Religious, Scientific and Spiritual Teachings, which explains from the outward the Esoteric Guidance Principle found not only in the hearts of believers but also promised in the deep spiritual teachings of all religions. This has to do with orienting our psychological preparation for the advent of Just World Governance.

The Future is Peace

(or there is no future)

The Future is Peace but it will not be gained by the power of war. All that the power of war will gain is death, Hellfire, and endless fear and military control with all its revolt, revolutions and rebellions, sleepless nights with endless fearful watchfulness, and endless terror.

If War is Hell, then Peace is Heaven, and that's where the real original Islam comes from, leads to, and means.

The choice is always ours, from moment to moment. If we suddenly discover that we've made a wrong choice, we must be courageous, rethink the placement of our will and make the right one. Here and now.

It is believed that the world effort to end anger and outrage has reached a sufficient momentum to succeed, and that the common understanding of these universal and religious goals by All involved will go a long way toward helping bring to an end the illusions of difference that fuel fear and anger.

To that end I wish to introduce the truth-concept of the Imperative of Spiritual Unity all peace workers may be familiar with the essential Unity teachings in all religions, but especially in Islam.

I hope thereby to show the English speaking Judeo-Christian world that the Peace, Faith and Fearlessness of the Muslim faith is the same as that being purported by the New Thought churches of Christianity,New Thought Judaism,New Thought Hinduism as well as the independent world class teachers and healers who are having such a profound influence on western philosophy and world success principles.

Similarly I wish to present a universally accepted understanding of the point and purpose of Islam, based upon my over forty years of prayer, contemplation, study and learning in association with some of the best minds of the contemporary Islamic world, the new age life coaches, self developement experts from around the world.

Unity (the Oneness and Uniqueness referred to as God) is Truth. The Unity or Oneness of God is the essential and central theme in all the teachings of Islam, and indeed, is the core teaching of all world religions(whether it is acknowledged or Not by the Hierarchy) spiritual and healing practices, and world-wide medical philosophies.

It is, in essence, the key to every success. Understanding it completely is the only real solution to personal and societal problems.

The key operative and motivational word here is "Success", which is what we all want (unless, of course, we're suicidal, and that will be dealt with elsewhere.

To the farmers, or peasants, because they work and harvest the earth, and thereby prosper.

The Muslim Call to Prayer, which is heard five times daily from every Mosque in the world. The first of the two Compelling Words in the call is "Salah", or "Prayer and Adoration".

One of the essential concepts to be understood is that among Muslims the acceptance of Jesus and Moses as true Prophets is an imperative as well as the 150 thousand Prophets that Allah(God) Almighty sent to different parts of the World over the centuries.

That the New current peaceful manifestations of those faiths are both worthy of respect and divinely inspired. That Logically and from a common sense point of view GOD does not need to beget nor is he begotten.

Most of my our work is dedicated to helping the Muslim world so that the angered and outraged among them will come to understand even more that the True followers of Original Christianity and Judaism (whose true numbers are hidden from the masses for fear of mutiny or revolt)of today per se are not enemies but friends and willing to help in the construction of a peaceful world and resolutions to all problems of territory and hunger.

In fact the last few verses of a Muslim daily Prayer is confined to Asking for blessings for Abraham's Decendents, which are the Jews and the Christians as well as the Muslims. Five times a day.

How would that knowledge change the Hearts of the followers of their Respective faiths towards each other.

Knowing that you are praying for your so called enemies because this is what God wishes for us ALL to do all the time.

To show love and compassion for all, Always and forever.

Original Islam in action

In true religion, there are no enemies. Our enemy is only within. If we learn to conquer anger and outrage we have won the greatest battle, called the Jihad al-Akbar in Arabic.

The idea is that anger and outrage are the real enemies of peace and the peaceful resolution of differences. How many times has the Prophet of

Islam (peace be upon him) insisted that restraint of anger was essential and a key to the development of both self-esteem and good character.

He also said that religion was for nothing if not for the development of noble character. He also said that religion was nothing if not wise counsel.

The following words are for the development of a truthful understanding of the reality and imperative of Spiritual Unity - why it is imperative and the consequences of ignoring this imperative for petty, personal gains.

It is hoped that these truth-concepts will contribute to the efforts of the New followers of the Original faiths, who are currently having such a wonderful balancing effect on the overall state of peace in the hearts of the world.

Translating the universal understandings to be found in the religion of Islam into a commonly understood English (or any other language) is the work of Muslims indigenous to that language and the work of Muslim travellers to foreign lands.

It is important to us all to have an in-depth understanding of the needs, goals and hearts of the people in whose land we find ourselves before seeking to teach.

We feel it our duty to help the people in whatever situation they find themselves, and at this moment the people of the world are struggling to understand Islam in terms that make sense to them.

All too often Islam, like many other faiths, has been used as a tool of subjugation by The followers who feel themselves also to be subjugated.

It is not for us to enter foreign lands as the missionaries of old, seeking to convert the people from their ways of assumed ignorance before truly understanding their natural quest for betterment of their lot and greater spiritual understanding.

Such activity is more like conquest than assistance. If we have the truth of God and the Reality of Surrender in our hearts, then we must see it in the hearts of others.

We must help them to see it and realize it in themselves. To understand our religion as a personal, inward manifestation of Gratitude and Surrender.

If we do not have it completely in our hearts, then we must seek first the complete understanding by associating ourselves with the true teachers of the way of peace,Afterall it's Very important that we follow Our beloved Prophet's Example of Always Keeping the doors to Beneficial Knowledge Open from Who ever and Wherever it comes as long as it benefits Allah's Wonderful Creations.

Not relying on fundamentals alone, completion of our own education first is mandatory, as well as, for the sake of unity, working in conjunction with already established peace teachers.

It is imperative for us to seek the reality and truth of religion not only for ourselves but to assist others in seeing it for themselves also.

This is done through human understanding and compassion, and not through presenting attitudes of contention and demand.

For all of us, it is imperative that we have a heart that can see and feel for the hearts of others. The sole purpose and first practice of the beloved Prophet Muhammad (pbuh), was to be a Mercy Unto All the Worlds.

Fulfill this and we have truly accomplished our goal, and all peoples will come to hear more of the teachings of True faith. We teach best by example, and our faith and way of life was sent solely for the development of noble character, to add to the peace and harmony to the world.

It is a religious imperative for Muslims to believe in the messages of peace brought by all the Prophets, including and especially Jesus, and we do.

His Second Coming is expected by us and it can be argued that it is now manifest in the resurrection of his teaching as found in the New Thought missions.

He and his teachings of truth are duly revered by all Muslims, and the purer the manifestation of his teaching by the people professing them, the greater the respect, understanding and cooperation that can be expected from the people of Islam and every other Faith.

After all, "Islam" is the imperative form of the word "peace", and is, in effect, the Command and the Way to Surrender.

This is the same Surrender that is taught in New Thought Christianity and is the prevalent principle in All Original world faiths.

Hence it is the Universal Salvation Principle, which is in keeping with the teachings of Islam.

If we now view the teachings of Islam as the Spiritual Psychology of this Surrender we are then Moving forward with our lives positively.

A way to further worship and gratitude for Surrendered people ("Surrendered" in Arabic is "Muslim"), then the study and understanding of the ideas and social practices of Islam will make much more sense to the West.

Whereas if we view Islam, as many of us do, as a religion of competitive demands, then its beauty, wisdom and guidance might well escape us.

Most Muslims understand both the spiritual implications of their religion and the commonality of their goals with the other faiths.

Followers of the original faith have carried and emphasize the true Prophetic practice of peace, mercy, and love that the Prophet, upon whom be God's Mercy and Blessings, imparted to a majority of his followers, who passed it along in private and in public, as circumstances allowed, throughout the generations.

Look at the History of Martyrs in All the faiths over the centuries and even the last 2 hundred years.

Wonderful souls who were persecuted by the hierarchy of their respective faiths for speaking against the

Confused and Manipulated beliefs of the faiths.

They were silenced once but their message of Unity was for the Truth to be heard by the True followers and achieve their real goal which was to Empower the Everyman over time.

To make people question,Doubt and Heal with True Unity.

The True followers of the One TRUTH are very highly educated in the spiritual implications of their religious teachings, have caught on stupendously in the culture of the more inquisitive mentality.

While it appears that a form of spiritual complacency has enveloped the majority of the Muslims, as a result of their choosing to view themselves as underprivileged and striving to "better" themselves materially.

The Qur'an states clearly why God chooses to withhold bounty from many, and it is exactly for fear of the mischief they might cause in the land.

It is for this that we must work to instill in the people of all faiths the feelings of unity, friendship, brotherhood and compassion, which to date had been the work of the inspired FEW in the World.

It now falls upon the many to properly understand the implications of the religion of Islam and the significance of the Spiritual Imperative and the common goal of all - that anger, outrage and aggression shall not rise again, and power, wealth and abundance may be fearlessly and gratefully shared.

Muslims,Jews,Christians,Hindus and all the people who seek Answers should not be too proud or arrogant to learn from others.

The Prophet (pbuh) taught that seeking knowledge is incumbent upon us from the cradle to the grave. He instructed us to seek it even if we were to travel to China. After all, it is our proven and historical practice to do so.

To facilitate this peaceSeekers must understand both the spiritual implications of their own faiths and the basic terminologies of similarity in the language of Islam.

World peaceworkers might also need to have some understanding of the sources of agitation coming from materialist interpretations of the religious teachings, which can sometimes lead ordinarily religious people to acts of anger, outrage and aggression.

Chapter Four

Embracing Bismillah Life Coaching

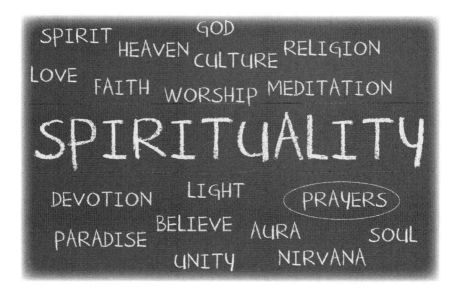

"WE" are immensely powerful people. "WE" can easily control the "world". Because in the moment we release our fears and transform ourselves into our capable, divinely empowered Selves, we release that same capacity into the universe and make it all the easier for others to do the same.

As the numbers increase, the Power of Peace spreads, and the fear and fear-based reactive mind and thinking dissipates and disappears.

"WE" (Ar. Nahnu) is the Mighty Name of Power that the Muslims claim exists in the secret realm. it is for this reason that Allah (God) in the Qur`an uses it to refer to Himself so often.

For "WE" are the Power of Allah, His Divine Representatives (khalifa) on earth. "WE" invite all around us to join us in heaven, and manifest it on earth.

There is a well-known Hadith (tradition in Islam) of common knowledge among Muslims that the last day shall not come until there has been forty years of peace and the sun has risen in the West. Need I say more?

THREE WORDS, THREE PRINCIPLES

Towards the Goal of Religious Understanding and World Peace and Unity

I'm not asking for Religious Unity because it already exists, but for Religious Understanding.

From Religious Understanding WILL arise Political Unity, because it is and will become truly evident that true religion (i.e. belief in One God) is the only real politic.

If the ONE -GOD conscious people of the world, who are by FAR, FAR, FAR the vast majority, continue in their demand for peace and freedom from tyranny,Emotional Blackmail on a huge scale from the hierarchy of World Religious Orders over centuries, which they will, then they must succeed.

There is an old saying in Sales & Retail Business that if you can find a need you can make the sale.

So there you have it,The reason for the attachments to God .

It's what we have been expecting and irrespective of whether the attachments may be a son, daughter or the sun or moon.

It's the fact that what seems abnormal over time with slow persuasion, some emotional blackmail, some physical pain examples shown to the masses(any one poor soul who feels he has a question would be dealt with in the best possible way to make the biggest, most fearful impact) and persecution in different guises.

The martyrs over the centuries From all the Main Controlling religions goes in to the millions and the numbers are still being counted.

There is no remorse for the casualties of war.

The war between Good and Evil has been claiming casualties for a long time.

Please make a choice that makes sense and at all times

Doubt

Question

Doubt

Question

If a faith is asking you to believe against all logic then question.

A friend of mine who is always sitting on a fence and always questioning, his favourite topic is religion asked a question.

When you say God is almighty, All knowing, All powerful, All Hearing, All Seeing Why do I need to go to a church/mosque/synogogue/halls/Temple for him to hear me or is the Transmission clearer from these places?

Great question.

Politics and religion have always been close allies.

The illusions, denial of the truth and politics have ruled the world rather than The undeniable Love of GOD throughout all of creation every second of existence.

Divide and Rule would be one answer I suppose.

Sometimes the answers are looking at all of us we just do not want to admit that we may have been took for fools and it is a lot less humiliating just to swallow whatever pride that leaves you with, keeping your head down is the safest bet for a lot of people.

Denial is sometimes the best bet or is it?

The one thing that will stop any internal feuding with other believing groups is a simple, unified, universal religious understanding based on three words and three principles.

Teachers will go a long way toward facilitating this Unity by incorporating this universally applicable understanding of three key Arabic words.

TOWARDS A COMMON RELIGIOUS VOCABULARY

Understanding the Meaning of Three Simple Words in Arabic and English

Al-llah! = The One, There Can Only Be One True Divinity, "The Oneness" and The Beyond Oneness, the Prajna Paramita of the Buddhists, that in which the Buddha dwells, the Tao of the Taoists, and that to which we are all surrendered, willing or not, and from which we all reap All our benefits for eternity.

There are two meanings to this Oneness, A) the undeniable Oneness or Unity of Existence, and B) the equally undeniable and ineffable Uniqueness of the Creative Force over and above the creation.

These two meanings are commonly referred to in Arabic as "Wahdat ul-Wujood", the Oneness of Existence, and "Ahadiyyat" The Divine Right of Uniqueness.

This is the same Oneness that the scientists observe, that the Taoists understand, that the Buddhists explore, to which the pantheon of the Vedas refer, and that all independent investigators discover.

51

We are either consciously aware of it or we are not. It is for each of us simply what is, and it is becoming obvious that it works for us to shift our love and attention to what is, otherwise we doom ourselves to always feeling "out of it".

So of this Oneness we can say, "love it or lose it". It is evident that we increase our intelligence, knowledge, love, wisdom and prosperity by staying in it. And we only increase our insanity by staying "out of it".

Al-Islam = "The Surrender" - that which we all know and do, even when we are not asleep like a baby.The Qur'an says we know this better than we know our own children.

Surrender is to our own inescapable Oneness in Existence and in recognition of the Uniqueness of The Divinity over it.

Surrender is to release our soul power and truly become all that we can be and are.

Muslim = "Surrendered" to the Oneness and the Uniqueness of God, Committed to the Surrender, and dedicated to PEACE ONLY, and to helping others.

I define Muslim as "liberated and fulfilled through being consciously Surrendered, and following an inner guidance toward a unified and benevolent self-governance for the benefit of All peoples".

This Surrender exists within us. So obviously people, when they are Surrendered, are already Muslim, or "in Islam", the State of Surrender, because that is the sole meaning of the word.

Our Beloved Prophet Muhammad (peace be upon him) taught simply that there are only two states (of being), that of Surrender and that of Conflict.

This is the teaching of Muslims that children are born in the state of Surrender, and that it is due to our environment and upbringing that we may leave it, and that it is our duty, quest and destiny to seek our way back to it.

It is in this sense that the Holy Qur`an refers to our beloved Jesus (`Isa, peace be upon him) as a Muslim (i.e. Surrendered to the Will of God), and that the way he taught and teaches - to enter into the garden, innocent as little children in the kingdom of God's forgiveness - is this very Surrender (i.e. Islam).

In this simple understanding of our Natural Surrender lies the Universal Reality of Religious Unity, and its Imperative. We ARE, innately, Spiritual Unity, and consciously IN Spiritual Unity when we are aware of our Surrender.

We are also in Political Unity when we become aware of our Surrender. With the awareness of this Political Unity, enforced by the natural Power of Peace (POP), comes the confidence of our success in the quest for A Unified World

Surrender is the Imperative. The choice is ours. It doesn't get any simpler than that.

So, now that we are all unified and on the same page, so to speak, we can begin in earnest our quest for A Universal World Guidance.

There are three simple principles to understand - The Imperative of Spiritual Unity, The Universal Salvation Principle and The Psychology of Surrender.

THE THREE PRINCIPLES OF THE POWER OF GUIDANCE

ONE - THE IMPERATIVE OF SPIRITUAL UNITY

The Reality of our Spiritual Unity is that we ARE Spiritual Unity.

The Imperative of Spiritual Unity is actually obvious. Without a recognition of Spiritual Unity in the outward through understanding and emphasizing the confluence of religious ideology expressed above.

we continue to have the illusion of differences in the outward, which we then continue to try to overcome or bridge, so we have no unity in the outward due to the fact that we don't recognize and honor the truth that we DO already have unity in the inward.

So first we must realize that our unity in the outward through Surrender to God is every bit as much a power and reality as our unity in the inward.

That we need to and are beginning to recognize it.

If there is to be peace, unity, and harmony, among the peoples of the planet, which exists already among the overwhelming majority, then this is the very peace, unity and harmony that must certainly be the main theme and teaching of all the World religions.

Therefore it is Imperative that we explore the power of our commonality in Surrender, not of our differences or superiorities, and make it the central focus of our teaching, because it is the reality, will be the reality and must be made the reality.

The Imperative of Spiritual Unity is exactly that, an imperative. We either recognize it, honor it and work within it, or we do not.

If we do, then we are surely in sync with Divine Purpose and assured of our success.

If we do not, then we are fractured, lacking in foresight and long-term confidence, and any successes achieved will be temporary, at best.

The Persian word for fractured is "Shikasta", and a well known writer wrote an incredible book by the same name on the fate of a planet that had broken its bond with the "Sense of WE Feeling".

It really is an imperative. We MUST - in the dual meaning of "absolutely need to" and "inevitably will" - surrender and come together in our oneness of Spiritual Unity.

All religions and Prophecies teach this, and the time is always Now. And for those who don't, well, we all make our choices and thereby choose our destinies.

The efforts that are presently being made in this direction are historical for Humanity. Never before has there been such potential for genuine change in the nature of World political thought.

Shifting Godliness and love of God into the political limelight is the work of All religions, and in one way or another, all spiritual paths.

The Misguided among all religions who have added partners to God over the centuries and have shaped God's character for Their Truths are just plain Dumb and many have been damned in the fruitless pursuits but have took alot of Very Naive souls who Simply turned their brains off, Accepted, Fell asleep, never to awake from the Illusions created by others they had put in charge.

Robots in Disguise found in all the different parts of the World throughout the centuries.

Converting ourselves first and then our family and friends to believers in the miracle of Surrender is the work we were all cut out for. It's innate within us. It's the work of true self-manifestation and the work of the truly Realized.

It is totally natural for us, once we have discovered this way of the peaceful heart, to want to convey its beauty and wisdom to those around us and to want to surround ourselves with fellow lovers of God, truth, self, healing and abundance.

Of course, to share it with the World, rejoicing in the discovery that many, many people know this already and are only waiting for us to call or to hear their call.

Surrender to Divine purpose is the known gateway to personal prosperity and World peace, both within our hearts and within our many mutual worlds.

Doing it (surrendering) on our own is the principle of doing it together.

Everything we want will come to us, quickly and easily through the immediately available Mercy of God.

The time is now for World peace and we know that God wants us to give up the endless struggle for personal prosperity in a seemingly hostile and objecting world, and accept it as the easy way so that we can get on with our real work of helping others.

Prosperity and Self improvement courses work because they are based on and convey this truth of ALL times. Make prosperity easy and you free yourself to do something with it. It's not so much what we do for our money as what we do with it.

Even for those who think that they do not have any, when they shift their thinking to "what am I doing with my money" (and my life), they will see all the answers.

God has made prosperity a key to our faith and easy for us for this very reason.

He wants us to devote our energies and our resources to other matters than our outward selves and our own personal security.

For professing Muslims, we are Surrendered and aware of our Surrender. We bear witness to our Surrender and to our awareness of our Surrender.

We bear witness to our need and gratitude for guidance and to our willingness to follow it wherever it manifests. We are saying all of that in our affirmation of the Unity of God and the Prophetic Guidance of Islam. This is the very bearing witness that we do in our daily lives and in our five times daily prayers.

Professing Muslims also claim that buried deeply within the teachings of our hearts in Surrender (Islam) can be found the perfect codes of personal behavioral social justice which, if implemented with dispassionate wisdom, can bring equity and harmony to Humanity.

Our quest then, is for the search and study of this code in preparation for its proper implementation at the hand of one trustworthy enough to be fair and just to all, even to the oppressor.

Merciless justice will never be supported by all, and if the world is to be a peaceful place, a belief in Merciful Justice must be established.

UNIVERSAL SALVATION PRINCIPLE

The Universal Salvation Principle is simply the Surrender. Allah says in The Qur'an that Surrender is the debt of nature, and the true repayment of the human debt of gratitude to God is to Surrender to God.

To seek and follow the guidance from God found among those who came before us in Surrender.

This is the Surrender of which I have written so much. It is the Surrender of the innocent or new-born child. It is the Surrender that the beloved Messiah proclaimed to be the key to kingdom of heaven (on earth).

It is the Surrender of the Muslims, the Christians, the Jews, the Buddhists, the Taoists, in fact of the ordinary person when he just plain gives up struggling.

It is the Surrender of the believer in "Let go, let God". It is the simplest thing that we do in the everyday realization of our lives and when we go to sleep at night. It is our inevitable destiny.

God did not create to punish, in spite of the fact that many people of faith believe otherwise due to their upbringing. People are born in innocence.

They do not have to accept any religion in order to go straight to heaven, but they may find themselves praying for wisdom and guidance in order to protect their innocence and that of their children.

People need only live lives of natural goodness, love, caring and compassionate behaviour.

Allah(God) Almighty is the only True Judge.

God is forgiving, again and again. It is natural, when we see we're doing something wrong, to turn to God and repent.

"I'm sorry, please excuse me, I won't do that again", means just that, in any language.

It is this Surrender that our beloved Prophet said children were naturally born into and their environment and upbringing made into them something different.

Surrender is the Universal Salvation Principle, and quite honestly, I doubt that any of us knows whether we will die in Surrender or not.

So who are we to judge others?

After all Just one great or just One good Act may very well change the course of Humanity and so it could go the other way as well.

Salvation and Prosperity. What a concept. It is the very definition of Heaven and the Essence of Surrender. In Arabic the word for Success is "Falah". It is the second Compelling Word in the Muslim Call to Prayer, which is heard five times daily from every Mosque in the world. It is singularly the most mysterious and alluring call in the human experience.

Everyone wants to know what it means. The first of the two Compelling Words in the call is "Salah", or "Prayerful Worship". Linking prayer and prosperity - doesn't that sound familiar?

THE PSYCHOLOGY OF SURRENDER

The Psychology of Surrender is simply that surrendered and happy people still seek company but with world peace/unity at the forefront in the minds all the time.

Once Surrendered we find ourselves curious and easily guided.

In fact, many people practice Surrender simply because they believe in and want to find and follow their infallible source of inner guidance But have not labelled it because they feel they should Keep it to themselves for The fears of Persecution .

Many have found it before us and claim that it will indeed lead us on the straightest path to our ultimate and most magnificent success but it Has to be a direct link with no interference, confusions, manipulations or treachery in adding other gods, idols in different forms that people have got so used to worshipping without realizing that they are replacing GOD-REALIZATION with what the World demands of themselves each second of their existence.

God knows that the Surrendered want and need guidance, both inwardly to their own best benefit, and outwardly to the perfection of humanity as a society, sharing in the abundant resources of a benevolent world.

Is that not the heaven that we are promised, or at least the taste of better things to come?

Is not the search for guidance one of the purposes of Surrender?

How could we heal the world without it? So on the next few pages I offer you the Heart and Soul of Islamic Eso- and Exo-terics on the subject of Universal Guidance.

The Unity of Religions, a Unified World Politics, a Vision of the Future, and the Search and the Preparation for the outward Manifestation of Our Inner Guidance.

As you will see, this is Our Universal Quest. This is the work in progress. But aren't we all?

ON THE IMPORTANCE OF THE CONFESSIONS OF TRUE FAITH

HEALTH, TRUTH AND SELF-VALIDATION

We validate Al-llah!, Al-llah! validates us

The most salubrious thing we can do is Affirm Truth. That's why a firm Knowledge of Truth is important to us so that we can avoid the affirmations of falsehood. And that's why the Quest for Truth is so important.

The most salubrious thing we can do is be in constant affirmation of the Reality of God, because God Himself is in constant affirmation of His Reality, and He affirms us as His Reality. So how much healthier can we ask to be?

However, it is no doubt that there is no end to the divine energy of God, but there must be some way to contain it in a proper manner, and a way to "harvest" it if you will.

Reciept and containment is through tramsmission and harvest is through worship.

Annihilaition is through remembrance. Annihilation is affirmation. Remembrance is affirmation. Affirmation of God is Affirmation of Truth and even though the ego is in search of its own annihilation, there is a more truthful part of us that will not be annihilated, not even by the 'fires of hell'.

That is the part that we will inhabit when all of the illusion is gone. That is the part that we will come to know and understand whether we want to our not.

So why should we not want to, if it's truth. If it is not truth it will disappear upon investigation, like all falsehood does.

Falsehood fears and flees from investigation because it does not want to be discovered.

It knows itself well, and feels itself purposeful and with intent, but knows itself to be but a cover-up for pain and fear and absence.

This is why only the courageous are on the pathway of self-discovery, just look at Histories of All the Religions and the Martyrs who gave their very lives to try to bring the truth to the people of their respective Times.

These are the reasons why constant connection with one who truly cares about TRUE FAITH is so important to the student of self .

There is also the element of community leadership.

Affirmation of Allah on a regualr basis at least five time a day by reaffirming True belief in and our unity with the Prophet (SAS)(peace be upon his name Forever)

A constant surrendering to God is a constant affirming of His Reality, and therefore a constant renewal of health.

Original Islam (surrender) brings everything that is good and nothing that is harmful.

THE END AND THE BEGINNING

Response and Unity for the ALL People FROM AROUND THE WORLD.

I would like to offer some possible assistance to the brothers and sisters seemingly frustrated with their FAITHS, looking for 'New Thought" in Islam/Christianity/Judaism/Hinduism and finding NO compassion or mercy they're looking for in one or another of the Unity Movements.

But unto that I say this:

Be Free to connect to ALLAH any time you please.

Do not wait for others to dial the number to connect yourselves to GOD-REALIZATION in everything in your life.

Islam means Surrender. It is the primary command of God. When we obey it we are Surrendered (Muslim) and in Heaven, and when not, not.

Belief in an ideology that makes one superior to others is childish ego-defensive sectarianism and not a part of the reality of Original true surrender, no matter how much they may protest against this.

One who has tasted True Surrender, knows.

Since profession or declaration of faith is the only requisite for full identification in Islam, I'm sure that none of the spiritually inclined populace of this or any other country will have any objection to sharing the declaration of spiritual belief held by the massive One GOD world in general.

Thereby declaring (again) the unity of humanity and the invitation to Know that common sense tells you that GOD ALMIGHTY does not need to share his Throne with any of his creation.

Does it make any sense at All to carry extra emotional bondage along all the other worries we carry with us in one life.

This declaration of faith, believed and understood without any objection by any Muslim sect or group, is simply and affirmatively that there is Only One God, actually nothing but God (la ilaha illa'llah - Only Oneness really Exists) and that this was the pure faith and profession of Abraham(peace and All our love be on him forever), Moses, Jesus and Muhammad(peace and All our love be on them All forever, all of whom were(their Original teachings are alive for the Real Truth-Seekers) and are the Prophets, the great teachers of and from this Undeniable Reality (along with Wise One God-Realized Martyrs from Varying backgrounds), and of the proper behavior patterns for the people of this Reality.

As Muhammad himself said this, it is summarized in Arabic by the second half of the Islamic message "Muhammadu-Rasulullah", Muhammad is (also) a true Messenger of this One Reality and the most important reality of Truth is that He was the FINAL Prophet sent to Mankind.

Forget the Imposters over the centuries who have duped an already gullible populace in to believing that they were the Prophets,Messengers or Saviours of Mankind.

Different parts of the world have suffered with these degenerated people who only want to have power over the people to stop them finding the truth.

These Twisted perverted people are the worst of mankind because they are the Devil's disciples but are cloaked in Disguises.

Their initial speech/smile will not give them away but if you ask the right questions they are seethingly angry and in all honesty would like to destroy you there and then, if they are allowed.

These people had/have a hidden agenda which they kept/keep from the masses and that throughout Disunity amongst Mankind has always suited their real master's purpose.

Look at the facts over time.

How history has been manipulated to suit the aims of the Few.

Why even the conspiracy theories are constructed to make the masses feel even more helpless than they already Feel.

A True Islam implies a constructive spiritual stability that is non-antagonistic and consoling to all peoples of all faiths.

In this respect it is perfect for the innate nature of the American people and European peoples, most of whom are naturally behaving according to the True Islamic principles of love and constructive cooperation so inescapable in our lives.

There's more, but there you have it.

Understood properly, this brief description of the problem, its origin and it's solution, often referred to in Islamic tradition as "The Sunrise in the West", should go a long way toward resolving, once and for all, any disputes that the wonderful people of Islam, my/our brothers and sisters, might have with their undeniable attraction to their own spirituality, which is indeed the felt call of God to Himself.

There Needs to be a Declaration of Unity through the different media resources we have at our disposal of the ONE-GOD Realized people from All around the world.

That would be truly historic and would go so far to bringing the World together.

To celebrate this unity and to feel Free of the chains of Man-made religion in all it's different forms.

Dearness to God: The Goal of True Belief

The Growth and Transformation of the BISMILLAH PEACE Movement

The flower children have reached maturity. The illusions of youth have long since passed, and the realizations sought after are being attained.

We broke loose in the 60's, studied and practiced in the 70's. Blended in and mellowed out in the 80's, and are rising by the power of Truth in Today's world.

The power of Truth with the help of You-tube,Face book,Twitter and the media, internet will transform the minds of all humanity to live a Heavanly life on Earth.

The information revolution has arrived and power of words will be truly felt throughout generations.

In the 70's Holistic Health was the study of physical disease and therapeutics. In the 80's it was patience, work and digestion.

The main thrust of Holistic Health in the present Day is spiritual realization as a means to personal and societal ideals.

Looking seriously at the realities of social reformation, spiritual truths have become the tools available for the attainment of personal goals.

Personal goals will include societal and environmental goals. Theology is a major force in intellectual and psychological reform and the studies and practices of the True faithful have risen as a means of understanding and achievement.

The Goal of BISMILLAH LIFE COACHING (Self-purification) is to understand and live in The True Love.

That goal, maintain the TRUTH FAITHFULLY, is the highest aspiration of the human heart. Love is the true force of creation. Creation is a manifestation of Divine Love.

Assuming that, let's explore the various meanings and manifestations of Love and their impact on the human individual and society.

We might define the basis of human motivation as "to love and be loved". The TRUE BELIEVER loves and is loved in the truest and ultimate sense.

S/he lives in the certain and experiential knowledge of God's Love for creation and humanity and therefore strives to know and become truly Human.

S/he spends his/her time doing deeds of self-effacement and purification, studying knowledges that will increase the orientation toward the One True Source and decrease the likelihood of falling into error and delusion, at the same time manifesting by every means available that same love in human understanding to all creatures.

By coming to know his/her own needs and the means to their fulfillment, s/he comes to know the needs of all humanity and the means to their satisfaction.

THE SEEDS OF BISMILLAH LIFE COACHING IN EACH PERSON,TO FEEL GOOD ABOUT YOURSELF THROUGH TRUE FAITH AND TO TEACH OTHERS NEAR OR FAR TO FEEL THAT WONDER.

THE MIRACLE OF OUR LIVES IS FOUND AND WILL BE ENJOYED BY A UNITED MANKIND EVERY SECOND OF Future EXISTENCE.

The Loss of Love

It certainly seems like the materialist society (whose goals are all the same) is simply putting the cart before the horse. We all feel the need for material stability, but why?

If we were to look deeply, we would find that we feel material stability would be an adequate (even requisite) platform from which to manifest and receive love - from family, friends and society in general.

The difficulty with this is simply that, as we all know, the life of this world is fleeting and thereby the search for material stability becomes all consuming and can lead to tragedy in virtually all areas of our lives.

The primary motivation (Love) becomes lost in the unending search for the unattainable, and never becomes attained. The goal becomes lost in the search for the means.

A man constantly caught in the quest for material stability will never have the time to love and receive love from his wife, family or friends.

This is the sad tragedy of the MODERN CIVILIZATION .

To this we say "Love Now!"

Put yourself right with Love. This is not an unpopular theme in the world of contemporary psychology. Let love flow from you now and you will discover from within yourself the very source of life itself, without which it is but a hollow shell.

You'll no longer be lost in the priorities of your mortal existence, and all self-concern or egoism will depart. This does not mean to say that you will become irresponsible.

Quite the contrary. You will fulfill your responsibilities all the more effectively since your motivation will be from the ease of love rather than from the hardship of concern and worry.

The Truly enlightened beings of the World have reached (at least) the stage of realization called 'Subsistence in Divine Love', and their only concern is to provide for their family (humanity) that same subsistence.

These wonderful Souls past, present and future are the Ones that keep the unity alive.

They may be of different origins, Backgrounds or social standing.

They may be Life coaches, Presidents, leaders of countries, Teachers, Scientists or a hundred other backgrounds.

They all have the unity of the whole Human Race deep within their very souls.

They Love God's Creation in all it's forms and are in constant affirmation of his wonders.

These may be people that go unnnoticed or are looked upon as a bit eccentric or Odd because they are always Positive .They have the connection to ALLAH ALMIGHTY.

Always showing compassion towards their fellow man, woman, child as well as any living creature.

Never judging but always Loving.

These are the people who may very well be the reason why the world is still here and not wiped out for it's insolent, ungrateful, arrogant behaviour Towards It's One True Creator ALLAH,He neither begets Nor is He begotten.

You could be one of them .

Hence their need to manifest. They possess a secret that wants to be known.

These Great Souls may be in Different walks of life.

From the Great life coaches,Mentors,Writers, leaders in Busines or politics to Ordinary people who may never achieve Worldly status but true respect they may find with ALLAH almighty in due course.

This level of existence is what we all aspire to. It is the aspiration and goal of the ORIGINAL RELIGION.

It is the ultimate and at the same time the beginning of "to love and be loved". To know and live forever in Divine Love.

A family, community or society based on such a principle is going to stay together through thick and thin.

You're never out of touch with Love

GOD IS KNOWABLE

What's more, Such as It is, Divine Nature makes Its knowledge incumbent upon creation. Ignore It at your peril. The good news is that it is possible. It would not be asked of us if it were not.

All words have meanings. All meanings are meant to be explored. Meaning is the source of knowledge. Knowledge is the understanding of meanings. Realization is the deep understanding of meanings. Meaning is that which is indicated (by a word). A meaningless word nullifies its own existence.

How does one explore meaning? With conviction, determination, investigation and repetition! The word 'Gnostic' means Knower (of God).

The word 'Gnosis' means Knowledge (of God). The word 'agnostic' means to be without knowledge (of God), and therefore, ignorant.

Consider, if you will, the meaning of the word 'ignorant' (Spanish/Latin: ignorante)- one who ignores. To ignore is an act of will and therefore of deliberate denial and uncaring, and therefore unknowing, (of the Divine Nature of Existence).

Now consider the consequences of ignorance - singularly the most damaging aspect of human existence. Fear, war, pestilence, disease, all the damaging elements arise from this one human quality .

The war of light is always with knowledge, against ignorance.

Consider the meaning of the word 'enlighten' - to remove the burden (of ignorance). Consider the meaning of the word 'wisdom' - the understanding and practical application of knowledge.

Do we know of anyone born with them? Are they not, then, noble objectives?

Consider the most fundamentally beneficial (and beneficent) aspect of human existence, the Knowledge of the Unity of us all.

Is not the Unity Beneficent? Contemplate Divine Unity for one moment and see what happens to you.

Is not this Unity sufficient to speak for itself? The slightest contemplation of it can be magnificently inspirational. Unity is the Source of Inspiration.

What is it that you listen to when you contemplate Unity?

All religious, spiritual and socially uplifting teachings are inspired by this Unity.

All religions, spiritual traditions, and ancient medical sciences and philosophies, from flower arrangement to homeopathy to the arts of war, include as an essential element a never-ending deep contemplation of, and listening to, this Unity.

Consider some alternatives. Would you support the contention that the Unity is incapable of speech? All of creation speaks to its kind and others in some form. Is not then speech an essential attribute of The Unity?

If capable of speech, would you consider It incapable of creating one (or more) able to listen? Who were the great spiritual leaders of history? All claimed the ability, by Divine Grace and Will, to speak for The Unity in the language of the people at that time.

Was not their message of eternal benefit to those who listened?

Should this Unity not have qualities that are beyond our comprehension? And should not this Unity be solicitous of our well-being, since It saw fit to bring us into existence in the first place? Is it not Aware, the Source and Author of a mother's love and a father's concern? Is this Unity not capable of creation?

Did we, and the creation of the known and unknown universes, past, present and future, arise accidentally, as though somehow without the consent, knowledge, cooperation and willful participation of this Supreme Oneness?

Can there be any thing greater than this Unity? Should this Unity be Knowing but not Conscious? We may have consciousness, but not that in and by which we exist?

Should not this Seeing, Speaking, Creating, Knowing, Willing, Compassionate, and Powerful Unity be able to give Itself a name and Presence unique to Itself in all languages.

That distinguishes itself from all previous concepts and misconceptions? And would you consider this Entity (Unique, Whole and One In Itself) unable to make this Name, and its Will and Purpose, known to Its creation?

Contemplate the meaning of these words! Al-lah! The One, greater than which there is nothing! Ahad! The Unique. Standing Alone, beyond comprehension, without necessity of Creation.

He is now as He was. Wahid! The Oneness, the Unity (Existing, Knowing, Seeing, Hearing, Speech, Will, Power), Who comprehends all.

The knowledge of Unity is a study; the Knowing of Unity is a practice. The Knowing and living in Unity is a primary obligation that supercedes all other obligations in importance and priority.

All action or non-action arising from this Knowing will be of the Source and successful. No other knowing can claim this.

One moment away from this knowing is damaging and to persist in its ignorance hardens the heart irreparably.

The Knowing of Unity benefits us in many ways.

   a)   Personally, with physical health and well being.

   b)   Socially, with a caring, unified society and the power of love and concern that such a society can bring to the individuals within it, and

c) Societally, by allowing the meeting of the races for the purpose of global harmony and balance.

This Divine Unity is the Source and Creator of all Sciences, foremost among which is the Science of Knowledge (of Divinity) itself.

Divinity has revealed the Science of Knowing. Divinity HAS made it available to those who would seek it.

It's called Gnosis, 'Knowledge of God', or 'God Realization' and is often referred to as 'the TRUE way'.

It has its roots in singular Truth and its origin in before time. The "Way" (to know God) has been espoused by every convinced individual from every religious and spiritual background.

What could be more practical, in any day and age, than the knowledge of the science of knowing the Divine Unity of us all? Divinity exists.

Even one's choice to ignore it affirms it. It is not erased from reality by such ignorance, only ignored.

Where does one go to seek knowledge of the Divine? Only the Divine can have complete knowledge of Itself, and only by Divine Will could Divine Knowledge be accessible to humanity.

The science/art of Perfecting Awareness

Bismillah Life Coaching

is Complete emergence of the principles of spiritual liberation and certainly famous for it's efficacy.

Liberation implies 'being set free'. It is not to be equated with rebellion, revolution or self-assertiveness. It can only be accomplished by an unconditional surrender, the reality of which must be tested. "call no man master lest he set you free."

This kind of spiritual freedom only increases the love, respect and service one has for one's teacher, much the same as one reaches maturity and goes about one's life independently never losing the love and respect for one's caring parents.

All spiritual traditions (religions) have their exoteric disciplines (practices) and their esoteric sciences.

These sciences have evolved like any others as a result of study and observation of the beneficial effects of devotion to the practice of the outward disciplines.

The true point of all religions is to provide a formula (teaching) and catalyst (teacher) for alchemy (the spiritual transformation of the student); the guided transformation of lead (the childish ego) into gold (the spiritually mature adult).

So all teachings must have their outward formulas, but without the chemist, the alchemist, the transformed teacher to act as guide, these laws are without reality, meaningless and ineffective.

Under mature guidance, Islam is a spiritually and socially transformative influence par excellence, and BISMILLAH LIFE COACHING will be widely known as an alchemy for spiritual evolution in every HOUSEHOLD whatever their Religious Background or past Mis-Conceptions about THE UNITY OF GOD(ALLAH) ALMIGHTY.

Logic Must Prevail and Common Sense Achieved.

The Perfection of Awareness

There are three stages to the perfection of awareness (at the end of which you are no longer aware, it is only Allah who is aware). They are:

Islam - Acceptance and Surrender (to the way of the peace and the love) - Surrender begins with the realization that guidance cannot be and should not be 'self-provided', that it must be sought at the hand of a realized spiritual Guide; and acting in accordance with that knowing.

At this point, according to your level of Himma (willingness), you will be put into contact with the NEW MODERN LIFE COACHING Islamic learning process.

Iman - Correct faith (with experientially verifiable certainty). The perfection of faith is its conversion to certainty (Yaqin) yielding correctness in behavior and knowledge coming from the complete realization of Truth.

A deep understanding of the human situation. This process has three phases: Hearing the Truth, Seeing the Truth, and Being the Truth.

`Ilm ul Yaqin - Hearing about this Knowledge. Knowing that there is a certainty. Seeking out and studying this knowledge.Realizing that there must be people and to be masters of this science and seeking them out.

`Ain ul Yaqin - Seeing the Truth, the Reality. Discovering the Source of Certainty. Coming into the presence and accepting the guidance of the people of this knowledge.

Haqq ul Yaqin - Being the Truth. Attainment. Becoming the reality (a carrier) of this Certainty.

Ihsan - Perfect guidance (finished, liberated, able to guide others). Spiritual Liberation implies the perfection of one's understanding of purpose and purity of intention.

It does not imply the kind of liberty that supports childish behavior and undisciplined carelessness, the contained and sober intoxicated; the TEACHER/LIFE COACH IN US ALL who is the union of the way of the walking (Shari`at - Muhammadun Rasulullah) and the Ultimate Reality (Haqiqat - La ilaha illa 'llah).

The completion of this process of alignment is the ultimate fulfillment and the end of personal desire. Thence the end of the ruling power of the perverse ego (both your own and others'), since ego is the defensive aggressive tool constructed for the purpose of attaining personal desire.

Personality is thence put to the uses that Allah intended for it in the first place, namely Compassion, service, friendliness,LOVE and education.

The Islam of the Modern Islamic Life Coach

In all my studies and travels, I have found no complete manifestation of the Islamic spirit anywhere except within the context of the ORIGINAL ISLAMIC PRINCIPLES. It was said by the Prophet that there would always be at least A BAND OF BROTHERS AND SISTERS FROM DIFFERENT NATIONS in whose hearts would be found the Reality of the Divine Message.

That these Beloved Souls will turn their backs on the imposters, charlatans, Manipulators of Religions who are the disciples of evil in disguises of Faith.

That these band of brothers and sisters will be articulate in Worldly affairs but their True devotion will be with the Truth of All Truths.

That they will be from different backgrounds but they will be united by the Truth.

Hallelujah Praise the Lord

Let us be thankful that there are indeed many more than that still available, and hope and pray that they only increase.

The spiritual stations, if not all the identities, of these people are known and talked about in Truly GOD CONSCIOUS Circles -- many of them are the recognized PIONEERS of any age and many of them are hidden from view and some of them don't know yet who they are.

BY PIONEERS I MEAN OF INDUSTRY, INVENTIONS, ENTERTAINMENT, CHARITY AND LEADERS WHO BENEFIT

THEIR FELLOW MEN/WOMEN/CHILDREN TO HAVE BETTER FULLER LIVES.

ONLY GOD CAN JUDGE, FORGIVE AND TRULY LOVE.

HUMAN BEINGS ARE LIMITED IN RESOURCES.

Bismillah Life Coaching is the science of divine realization within the Islamic context, we emphasize 'within the Islamic context', but stress that this 'Islamic context' is defined in the heart of the Truth seekers.

Massive portions of Islamic knowledge can be learned from books. The libraries and bookstores are full to the brim with contemporary and ancient literature on the subject, and there seems to be no end to the number of seekers in the World today From Every corner of the Planet.

They may not be Recognized as such but ONE GOD-REALIZATION is their Ultimate Goal.

However it must be realized that the realities and arenas for the practical application of these knowledges cannot be found in books, indeed the best possible description of these realities is that they cannot be even described, let alone transmitted, through writing. Service and seeking, are for the most part forgotten sciences.

Please recognize and honor the true purpose and benevolent nature of the Islamic revelation. This understanding is a prerequisite to your SALVATION.

For without believing in the Benevolent Nature of The Divine and by extension, the Prophets, books, and revealed lifestyles, one would have no reason to accept the teachings of a PROPHET hence no reason to apply oneself to membership in a TRUE ISLAMIC community.

If we do recognize the nature and purpose of the Divine Message, then we will have no difficulty in recognizing the benefit and blessing both to ourselves and to humanity in general, derived from seeking out and applying ourselves to the services, studies and practices indicated by these TEACHERS OF MANKIND PAST AND PRESENT.

That does not mean that you need a sign to say who you are and what you believe, that is your personal relationship with GOD Almighty.

Chapter Five

The Powers of Bismillah & Surrender

Surrender to Allah (Islam) implies limitless freedom, while subservience to the self and its personal concerns guarantees endless slavery.

Illusion is deceptive. That is its very nature. A well-known maxim among the TRUTH SEEKERS is that 'the gates of paradise are surrounded by the fires of hell, and the gates of hell are surrounded by the temptations of paradise.'

If one sees the fulfillment of one's personal ambitions as the ultimate goal of life, (i. e. the illusion of paradise), and that their dead sacrifice in the service of other-than-self is what is being asked of them in exchange for true personal and spiritual fulfillment, one can get a taste of the meaning of this maxim.

The Prophet said that he (and Islam) would always be found among the poor. This implies also that many of the rich will be too hopelessly under the sway of fear for loss of what they had gained of worldly wealth and position to be able to offer the surrender and help necessary for the attainment of true spiritual service. Also that among the poor would always be where the service was needed.

WHY THE RICHEST PEOPLE IN THE WORLD ARE LEAVING ALL THEIR WEALTH TO CHARITY

There have been many very well-to-do individuals throughout history who have realized the benefit of either leaving or offering their wealth and service for the cause of spiritual and social benefit.

Working with All communities for the One community.

In Reality nothing is lost. But the social harms and personal dangers that are caused by clinging to a limited, personal concept of life and material substance are extremely evident contemporarily and historically.

The real distinction is between slavery (to everything: self, desire, worldly life, and temptation to evil), and freedom (liberation from said slavery) to serve transcendent goodness and help in the liberation of others. Hence the famous statement "'If you are not part of the solution, you are part of the problem'"

Barakah - The Magnetic Dynamics of the Blessing

(Barakah = Love, Blessings, Divine Grace, Good Karma, the Substance of Compassion)

Whether you know it or not, The Divine (Allah, God), in Wisdom, is the Master of All Hearts, and by extension all else within the human existence.

The Divine that places love in their hearts by allowing it to grow in stages after allowing the always present seed of Peace to take root.

Peace is one of the fundamental natures of The Divine Reality.

It is by the Love and feelings of attraction that peace produces that sufficient continuity is provided to allow the learning process to take hold and flourish. In other words, if you did not like the feeling you get from being around someone, you'd not have the patience or inclination to learn from that someone.

It is only from within the security of an established bond of trust that personal or painful subjects may be allowed to emerge.

Often we may find ourselves investigating the presence of someone who is espousing the most desirable principles, but in our hearts we know that this particular person is not for us.

BISMILLAH LIFE COACHING invests true teachers with three fundamental qualities -- they are not boring, they take your burdens from you, and they speak what is in your heart.

These sensations are all coming from the heart of the student, and it is Allah that is placing them there. It is the heart that is seeking for resonance (open to Unity) that will be responsive to Allah's guidance when it has found it. That's Barakah!

The nature of God and the nature of creation are so vast as to be invisible and thereby incomprehensible. This incomprehensibility is the reason for the obligation upon The Creator to provide guidance.

Creation and all its aspects are from the Rahmah (Mercy) of Allah. This includes, of course, free will, or the ability to choose, which implies the necessity for all the equally alluring opportunities for wrong-doing, and therefore the necessity for the presence of temptation to evil, the benefit of which is only in its repulsion.

Facing, turning toward with healing love and benevolence, or Divine Attention, is the primary response of Al-Rahim. This is why we begin everything with 'Bismillahir-Rahmanir-Rahim'.

The first thing we do with this invocation is invoke the Name of the ESSENCE of the Essential Being, That without Which there would be nothing, but Which would exist anyway. The Manifestor without manifestation; Allah, The Divinity, Being as It was before Creation, So is It now and So will It forever be.

Next remembered is the Nature of His Intention for Manifesting, Benevolence.

Completion of the invocation is with the remembrance of His Foresight and Responsiveness to Individual Needs; the Nature of Personal Attention from The Divine.

Hence the Divine purpose of giving us this invocation is to cause us to remember the Essence, Allah, His intention, the Manifestation of Divine Benevolence, and the personal effect of His remembrance, i. e. personal attention in the form of Peace, patience and the fulfillment of your needs.

In other words, to attract more (open yourself up to the realization of) Divine Attention. The palpable, acquirable and dispensable manifestation of Divine Attention is known as Barakah, and is commonly felt as Love.

We begin with the invocation of Allah, opening ourselves to His Existence, Help and Guidance in all our endeavors, large and small.

We realize that we are totally dependent upon Allah for our very existence, and upon the Mercy and Wisdom of Divinity for our situation in Allah's Magnificent and Benevolent Creation. Ya Rahman.

By the invocation of the name and attribute Ar-Rahim, we are consciously supplicating (requesting) the Divine Grace (Barakah) that He knows we need in order to be successful and guided in this life.

We are affirming that He knows what the true success is and He knows what we need by way of guidance and willingness (Himma) to follow it. So our intention (niyyat) with this invocation is to ask for Surrender to Allah's (Divine) Will (Islam), because Allah is Knowing ('Alim) and we are not.

For this reason and in response to this request, Allah sends to us and to all humanity the universally accessible guidance of Islam,Over the centuries to different people, through many languages, different continents, in various guises with compassion, which means primarily "Surrender to Divine Will" and implies secondarily "acceptance of Islamic (human and humane) principles and lifestyle".

He does this that we may receive and dispense Divine Grace (Barakah) and become fully realized and functional human beings and intermediaries with a heart in heaven (the next world, al-akhirah) and feet firmly on the earth (in this world, ad-dunyah); in other words, THE TRUE MUSLIM(One who is surrendered to Almighty God-realization), before the rise of the agent, middleman, arbitrator or the mischief maker to spoil mankind's direct relationship with his Creator)

If we seek it, Allah will gift us with the understanding to embrace Islam properly, that we are not to be led astray by our own misunderstandings from its True Source and Proper Purpose.

For the purpose of this guidance and true understanding Allah has guaranteed us the existence of a certain minimal number of TRULY GUIDED UNSELFISH SOULS(who may or may not be what you expected) with both outward and inward proofs that are convincing enough, to which we may be drawn, insha'llah (if Allah wills).

These wonderful souls have a connection with their creator and are ready to share that connection.

TRUE MUSLIMS begin their praises with Bismillahir-Rahmanir-Rahim and end with the praise of Him from Him, "Al Hamdu lillahi `ala Ni`matul Islami wa kafa biha ni`mah. " "Praise be to Allah for the favor of Islam and it is a sufficient favor."

Bismillahir-Rahmanir-Rahim

For the FAITHFUL, all things begin and end with the name of Allah. So the first phrase from the lips of the FAITHFUL is

Bismillahir-Rahmanir-Rahim. Meaning - beginning with the Name (and thereby, hopefully, with the Remembrance of the Truth and Reality) of Allah (God), The Compassionate, (Whose Compassion extends to all creation, comprehensible and non-comprehensible, and all creatures, no matter how near or how far), The Merciful. (Whose Mercy is available to all who supplicate).

All praise is due to Allah (God), who created with no diminishment of Divine Resource. Who supports His Creation without expending any strength, and Who allows it to continue for an appointed term, that His Purpose might be accomplished.

He needs not do this at all, but for His pleasure, and that He, in all his Might and Glory, might be known by his Creation. And Glory be unto Him, Who in His Wisdom, created mankind of a living animal kind, and placed upon his head the crown of Reason, and into his heart, the essence of His Love.

Glory be unto Him, Who is high above all that is attributed to Him. And May His Divine Peace be upon all of His messengers, and all Praise and Gratitude is due unto Allah (God), Lord and Creator of ALL Worlds.

The understanding of the subtle distinction between the generally operational mercy and the direct personal attention from the Divine Reality is represented in the Bismillahir-Rahmanir-Rahim. The Rahmah of Allah is such that existence exists, people exist, and equal opportunity to do good or evil with one's life exists.

It is such a general and diffuse and easily (even unnoticeably) available form of mercy and understanding that mankind is easily misled into thinking that he need only seek out his own personal well-being and that that is all there is to life.

It is also so comprehensive as to include within itself the aspect of responsiveness (al Mujib), and guidance (Al-Hadi) and this personally responsive aspect of Ar-Rahman is Ar-Rahim.

The nature of God and the nature of creation are so vast as to be invisible and thereby incomprehensible. This incomprehensibility is the reason for the obligation upon The Creator to provide guidance. Creation and all its aspects are from the Rahmah (Mercy) of Allah.

This includes, of course, free will, or the ability to choose, which implies the necessity for all the equally alluring opportunities for wrong-doing, and therefore the necessity for the presence of temptation to evil, the benefit of which is only in its repulsion.

While the general diffused, equally everywhere existence of Rahmah, or Divine Benevolence, available equally to the good and the bad alike, is the observable manifestation of Ar-Rahman and the Overall Mercy from which creation springs, its magnetic aspect, its specific, individually responsive nature is called Rahimiyyah and its palpable manifestation is called Barakah which can actually be accumulated with no depletion or shift in its original source.

It can also be dispensed, and that is the work of the TRUE FAITHFUL MUSLIM, particularly the TEACHERS. A major carrier and manifestation of Barakah is Knowledge (`Ilm), both outward and inward. Another is Presence.

Rahmah, or Divine Benevolence, is the source of what is known to us as Universal or Unconditional Love and Caring. Rahimiyyah is its responsive nature that pours out very careful and personal attention upon them who supplicate or seek.

Rahmah is the supportive creative ingenuity and reliability of the good man and devoted father, Rahimiyyah is the caring love and consistent personal maternal care of the good woman and devoted mother to her immediate family. Neither is exclusive to the other.

Next remembered is the Nature of His Intention for Manifesting, Benevolence.

Completion of the invocation is with the remembrance of His Foresight and Responsiveness to Individual Needs; the Nature of Personal Attention from The Divine.

Hence the Divine purpose of giving us this invocation is to cause us to remember the Essence, Allah, His intention, the Manifestation of Divine Benevolence, and the personal effect of His remembrance, i. e. personal attention in the form of Peace, patience and the fulfillment of your needs.

In other words, to attract more (open yourself up to the realization of) Divine Attention. The palpable, acquirable and dispensable manifestation of Divine Attention is known as Barakah, and is commonly felt as Love.

Invoking the name of Allah satisfies a primal and general religious requirement to begin everything in the Name of God, the reward of which is no small thing but in truth depends upon your intention.

Secondly, and depending upon your level of awareness (which increases with study), it brings to mind and to heart the awareness of the Reality of God with the invocation of the name of Allah alone.

Then with the invocation of the name and primary, all-inclusive attribute Al-Rahman, one is reminded of the Source of Creation and the infinite and benevolent nature thereof, as well as of the endless oceans of Universal love .

The Practice of Remembrance (Dhikr)

There is a science to the use of the names of God (Allah) in Arabic. It is one of the spiritual subtleties of the science of remembering our Reality.

Although the true gnostic (realized knower of Divine Reality) knows what s/he is referring to with the mention of the word 'God', there is not yet in the English language a science to bring that realization fully home to the unaware seeker.

One of the true bases of TRUE ISLAMIC practice is exactly this science.

Compare simply the effect of repeating the word 'God' over and over again to the effects of repeating the name 'Al-lah'. Sufficient repitition causes one to think about and hopefully know, what one is saying.

It also has the effect of knocking at a door until it is opened. This effectiveness of repitition holds true for all of the Arabic Names of the attributes of the Divine Reality and is another manifestation of the science of Gnosis (awareness).

If we were to discover that one practice 'works' and the other doesn't, or that one method is manifestly more 'effective' than the other, what we would be comparing is the awareness received.

In English these Divine Attributes are objective descriptions, i.e. nouns and adjectives, and truly meaningful only to the gnostic who has already attained an inner realization of True Meaning.

There is of course some benefit from the contemplation of the meanings of these words, but there is no real established science for total realization using only the English language.

There is, however, such a science in Arabic, and this is the science of Dhikr (remembrance) as revealed by the Prophet Muhammad and taught by the TRUE FAITHFUL TEACHERS.

It is said that when man remembers God, God remembers him. It is from this remembering by God of man that he knows his True Reality, and it is this true reality that constitutes the basis for true self-knowledge.

The journey to and through the self can be long and arduous. Without proper orientation, guidance, tools, and knowledge of how to use them, it is impossible.

That it IS possible at all comes as good news to man, for no effort is too much in the quest for escape from darkness and the plentiful reward of light and guidance from the Divine.

It is helpful for us to think of the journey in terms of stages of awareness. For the traveling through these stations we have the teaching of the FAITHFUL TEACHERS OF THE TRUTH.

It is not recommended to attempt this journey without a guide, and the teachings of the guide of this age can be obtained from any of his students.

It is said that to attain a moment of PURE contemplation is WORTH a life time of worship! To know Objective Reality we must have a sign (ayat) to contemplate, a Truth by which we may be guided.

For the Muslims, this Objective Reality, and the path to it, is indicated by the "Kalimah Tayyibah" (Finest Words).

La ilaha illa 'llah, Muhammadun-Rasulullah

La ilaha illa 'llah, Muhammadun-Rasulullah

For the TRUE MUSLIM, the most meaningful words in creation are "La ilaha illa 'llah, Muhammadun-Rasulullah."

We claim unequivocally that this phrase is the Origin of all Knowledge, the Sum of all Meaning, the Source of all Truth, and Health, Warmth and Healing to the heart.

Let's examine the phrase in its two components, *"La ilaha illa 'llah", and "Muhammadun-Rasulullah"*.

Part 1. La ilaha illa 'llah

"La ilaha illa 'llah" is the essence of the matter, a simple but profound summary of the "Knowledge of God". It is the essence (and practice) of the annihilation of falsehood. It is both a statement of Divine Truth, and a lesson on how to know it. It means that there IS ONLY Allah, and demonstrates that the quickest way to "know" the Unity is to deny all else.

"La" means no, nothing, negating of what follows, indicating the negation of and implying the illusory nature of the seeming existence of whatever it is referring to, (which, paradoxically, must first "exist" (in the mind) in order to be negated, denied, refused, diminished to zero relative significance).

"Ilaha" is an intensely interesting word, worthy of deep consideration. It means god (little 'g' intended), deity, worthy of worship, deification, edification, respect, subordination, following, service, attendance, consideration. In a word, just about anything that comes from our (individual) minds (mindset, way of thinking), and anything we might care about (our cares), or believe "exists".

"La ilaha" can therefore mean "nothing exists", i. e. nothing is worthy of consideration except that which stands by itself and is not in need of consideration.

How do we isolate that Being? By eliminating from our consciousness (mind) all that can be eliminated, even and including all mental concepts (of God), until there is only pure existence itself, pulsing through our bodies and flowing through our veins.

The indication is that the "Knowing" of God is based on the negation of all else. In practice, that negation is based on an exclusive affirmation of The Only Possible Permanent Reality, God Alone. Once the "Knowing" is known, it stands alone and sufficient. There is no more negation necessary or even possible, and everything becomes an affirmation of the Truth in Reality.

In ISLAM, the word "annihilation" refers to the mind (giving no credence to). There is no denial of the outward existence, only the negation of any reality other than the Only True Reality (That which is left when all else is gone). Look how even the basest tyrants act according to this law, seeking to physically destroy their enemies and succeeding only at self-ruin. Nevertheless the principle is the same - arriving at the truth by a process of elimination.

"Illa" means only, but, if not, except.

"'llah" means Allah, Al-lah! (Arabic) The One. The Conscious Oneness. The Unity. The Divine, The Beyond-Comprehension. The Self-Aware, Who Comprehends All. Existing, Knowing, Seeing, Hearing, Speaking, Willing, The Source of Power. Perfection in and of Itself. Greater than which there is none.

Who remains when all else is gone.

This Existence must be both intellectually grasped and physically realized. The Divine "Does" Itself. The full embodiment of the Reality of this Truth is the object in "Quest". Knowing it in our minds may be easy but convincing our bodies takes practice, including verbal affirmations and physical negations. This practice transforms this knowing from a concept to a reality.

Part 2. Muhammadun-Rasulullah

Muhammadun-Rasulullah is a profound summary of the knowledge of creation.

"Muhammad" is the most complex and meaningful word, requiring the study of long eulogies for initial comprehension, so let us summarize. He was indeed the full embodiment of Truth and The Reality, and therefore the way for us to attain a Very High standard of Truthful everlasting Qualities.

Rasul means messenger. Messenger implies way. Message is the teaching, Messenger is the way. What the messenger can do, the receiver of the message can do. Implying coming from and returning to the Source of the message. In this case, Allah. 'ullah means to confirm that - (messenger) from Allah.

The Realms of Existence and the Attributes of Essence

The Supreme Consciousness - The Existence of Divinity Independent from and Indifferent to Works (of creation).

The uncreated Ultimate Reality. Allahu Ahad, "The very 'stuff' from which everything else is composed". Allahu Samad - "Yogic scientists have long said that the ultimate cause of all existence and the source of all material objects can be nothing other than pure consciousness."

The Essential Attributes (Sifat udh-Dhat) are Seven. These are the Inherenent Attrributes of Divinity independent of works.

Existence, Knowledge, Power, Will, Sight, Hearing and Speech.

The Realm of God relative to His works, pertaining to His Dominion and Power (to create). He would not be "God" if He were not worshipped, reflected in and by His work. "He became 'God' when He decided to." Part of the 'created' realm.

Energy, "The Compelling" - the Will of God, The "Force", The Supreme Power - the Used Potential - of Divine Intention.

The Reality of the Divine Ideation - The Thought of God, the Overall Plan, The Spiritual Truth and Reality of God's Creation.

Energy Healing in the Original Islamic Way

Set against the backdrop of the Unchanging, or 'no change',BISMILLAH LIFE COACHING is the science of change. It is the journey (should you choose to accept it) of the personal truth (subjective) toward the absolute truth (objective). It is the science of the subject's approximation to and eventual annihilation in the object.

It has been said by many of the Early Faithful followers that Soul purification was a reality without a name, and in the latter days it has become a name without a reality. It means self-purification. It is an event.

It is what happens (by the permission of Allah), when one accepts and walks the revealed Way in Surrender (Islam) under the guidance of a mature and spiritually authorized teacher.

Therefore, in the early days it was a reality without a name.

In the ensuing attempts to spread Islam by the heart, which was it's original and only intent, only mature faithful followers were sent into foreign countries to assess and blend in with the people at their level of understanding and adapt their presentations of the teachings to acceptable standards.

They would become, in all outward aspects, one of the people but the superiority of their moral and ethical virtues would shine forth in an exemplary manner and have a transformative effect upon the populace.

Hence the teachings spread. . It is the science of transforming undesirable qualities into desirable qualities.

In this context, only what works, works. Only what works is real. And it must be tested on the touchstone of practicality.

It is stated in tradition that the earth would never be without a unique individual who would be the standard by which success was measured. It is the obligation of all who accept obligation to continue the search for this unique being within us All because he is the center of unity and holds the key to the unity of the people, without which there is no real and practical outward unity. He is the fountain of love, wisdom and mercy for all the Worlds.

This time is no different and we are blessed, as tradition states, to see the spread of Truth and the emergence of an increasing number of qualified teachers,Life Coaches and Mentors who have True love for the Good of Mankind and who are for the most part of ONE GOD Faith.

Among the saints, teachers and holy people there is an order and a unique being from whom pours forth the love, mercy and wisdom in a way unique to the time, much needed by the others regardless of their station in life.

The Bismillah Life Coaching schools will be established by this universal desire of mankind to find the innate reality always revolutionary and new in a way that truly fits the place and the needs of the people of the time Anywhere in the World

You Are Worthy to ask God for anything GOOD and PURE, do not be shy.

Bismillah Life Coaching is not an unknown phenomenon in western culture.Life Coaches and Healers abound. Prayer, contemplation and introspection, spiritual and behavioral transformation are the hallmarks of this spread, and may well be the salvation of the Universal dream.

Major curiosity has always been present concerning the usefulness and means of blending and incorporating western understandings (particularly psychology) into the True original Islamic way.

It has always been a part of the True way to accept and integrate the contributions of the people to whom it was brought. Common examples are Unani (Greek) medicine, Indian music, Buddhist meditation and Malaysian martial arts, to mention a few.

These incorporations always met with resistance from some among the more traditionally oriented populace.

For Islam to be truly accepted and Unite the World, the contribution par excellence and most needed is the spiritually adaptable portion of Human psychology which has explored itself to the depths of the human spirit much the same as physics has come to the point of having to accept a Supreme Being.

It is now time for our spiritual tradition to arise and embrace the transformative works of the people who have strived to the best of their ability to understand and relieve the sufferings of ALL people.

Working with All communities for the ONE community.

To meet and offer itself as the natural continuation to The work of the True Islamic Jihad of Muhammed (peace be on his beautiful name forever) TO BRING UNITY AND LOVE AMONG ALL OF GOD's CREATIONS.

Although it can, Original True Islam is not meant to 'stand alone' as a panacea to the world's problems. It is not meant to be introduced as a cultural alternative, as in simply adopt a new cultural, in this case Islamic, paradigm, and allow the rest to sort itself out.

It is meant to be dynamically unifying, embracing and meeting the needs of the people at their level of understanding.

True Islam as an 'alternative' movement creates separation and becomes a practice without a heart, or with a 'heart' of it's own.

In order to be a living, dynamically transformative force it must be able to enter almost unnoticed into mainstream life; accepting and transforming, for example, the music, the corporate business practices, and the next generation of healing arts such as Life coaching, Soul Healing and yoga.

There is no doubt that the plethora of True Islam today are holders of very high spiritual stations and are sufficient for the seekers of spiritual realities and for the salvation of their adherents.

They offer the vehicle of Islam as a way 'out' of the dangers of contemporary life.

The heart of Islam is the reality and practice of spiritual transformation; discovering, understanding and implementing the practical means by which tangible results are achieved.

However in most cases it is then left to the student to do the 'walking' (studying, learning, etc.) by himself, since, even though the stations of the way may be known, without the deep understanding of the love and the mercy, students are largely left to the discipline of self control rather than to the freedom of self transformation.

The acceptance of Islam alone is sufficient to heal through the commonly understood principles of behavioral (energy) modification.

The Law of Attraction kicks in By correcting and aligning one's actions, speech, and thoughts (energies) with the Divine plan, one alters the course of one's life, and changes its direction from degenerative and destructive, to regenerative and constructive.

This is a most fundamental form of energy healing.

Not to mention the fact that true Islamic Students have always been blessed with the key to energy healing. It is meaning and implying - to face with intent or intention, to pay attention to or send energy (or love) towards.

It is noted in many treatises that this power was exclusive to <u>original Truth inspircd followers </u> and that there was no mystery that it was a dispensation from the Divine; a sufficient portion.

The dynamics of this marvelous phenomenon are amply clarified by the Bismillah Life Coach.

The realization of the power of the subconscious mind and link with the soul opens doors for All to learn more and become Life coaches in their Homes, social circles and communities/cities/countries.

It does not matter about the age of the life coach or whether male or female, as long as the love of Allah is within their hearts along with a passion to make a positive impact on their lives aswell as others.

What a Wonderful thought.

These evidences should be sufficient to satisfy any doubts as to the necessity of energy healing as an integral part of contemporary ISLAM, and as to the role of Bismillah Life Coaching in the revival of this wonderful science.

The Healing Power of Conscious Recognition leading to cement subconscious positive habits for a truly satisfying pure life with real Productivity.

It has been my experience that nothing heals as well as conscious recognition, and that nothing heals completely without conscious recognition.

Most of healing is dealing with the consequences of unconscious behavior.

Looking at Your life from outside the Box or seeing it as a Ongoing Film with full glorious colour for the Big events and possibly black 'n'white for sombre or sad moments.

A lot of big budget films have 4-5 different endings and a Director's cut.

So what ending would you like to Give your film.

The art of healing is the art of correcting the underlying assumptions that are the causes of unconscious behavior. It is complete when understanding and forgiveness set in.

Energy healing is a pathway to the discovery of truth. When causes are recognized, behavior can be corrected and lessons learned. In order to effect a complete cure we must discover true causes and bring them into conscious recognition.

Visualization is another practice which is integral in the healing process which is the process of seeing yourselves in Positive Action and seeing your life unfolding with True Surrender to Allah as The Fountain from which all Great Things Spring.

Visualization is a process that through practice can develope alongside Positive affirmations can build a confidence fortress against depressive or Degenerative behaviour for the student, young or old.

Infact the earlier in life the better.

The purpose of a manifestation (symptom) is to draw attention to its source. Energy healing is a way to investigate a manifestation (consequence) and arrive at a clear recognition of cause.

Learning the lesson (i.e. seeing the truth of the situation) brings relief and gratitude, and wounds serve their purpose and may heal.

Gratitude for the healing, and the lesson learned, allows for the process of forgiveness to begin.

From the position of relief and gratitude, one may come to an understanding of the distorted motivations that brought about the wounding, and even the causes of these distortions.

At which point the forgiveness of deep understanding sets in.

A deep understanding of the causative emotional disturbances will almost always reveal how they were motivated by a distorted interpretation of love, either the desire for it or the desire to express it.

From that understanding, forgiveness may emerge.

The point of spiritual practices and techniques is the release of our Divine Awareness from the clutches of emotional bondage.

Emotional bondage (attachment) is the root cause of resistance, and these emotional bonds are located deeply within our subconscious.

It is this emotional bondage that impedes our bodies from complete surrender to the happiness of the soul.

When the body is surrendered completely, the soul is then free to explore the treasures of the heart.

That's where the happiness of life begins.

To embody Divine qualities is to allow them to flow through us unfiltered and uninterpreted.

In order to do that, total surrender is required.

Energy healing is a process of identifying and locating these emotional bonds, most of which are in the form of hidden associations with the past. Bringing them and their causes into the present (conscious recognition) is the means by which they are released.

Bringing our emotional wounds into conscious recognition, understanding their causes and the compulsions caused by them is the means by which they are healed and appropriate behavior is restored, once and for all.

The only thing attempting to prevent us from doing that is our fear of them.

Real understanding begins with a compassionate interest and the knowledge that underneath every Dominating Energy (or act of frustration) there is a responsible cause that is fundamentally benevolent and healing in nature.

We might even call this the "Primary Understanding".

Deep down, every person seeks understanding. True understanding can be felt, and the inner being receives it as vital help and as the necessary prerequisite to being helped, and all of us are needing and hoping in our heart of hearts to be helped.

Receiving help is self-affirming - it is validating of life-efforts. In other words, it helps us to heal our hearts and prepares us to pass it along. Receiving help affirms our understanding and thereby our goals and sense of rightness.

We are all struggling for success. Having a really clear understanding of the honesty of our true motivations and a compassion for the needs of humanity is a means of achieving success.

If we can know and manifest the truly benevolent nature of our own motivations, then we can help others to find theirs. So being understood is a prerequisite to being helped, and we all need help. This is truly Original ISLAMIC WAY and The HUMAN Way thereby The CIVILIZED way.

It's the right thing to do. Healing and learning to heal is the appropriate behavior of the age. Why do we behave the way we do? And why is our behavior degenerative instead of regenerative?

A successful life is based upon appropriate behavior. It is therefore appropriate behavior for ALL societies to learn how to repair and heal the consequences of its own inappropriate behavior.

This is true repentance (rethinking).

Application for Rethinking available to All of Humanity with No Discrimination.Even the people of religion who feel they have one foot in Heavan should Rethink.

In the safety of a sacred friendship, we may ask to be shown the secrets of our hearts, to purify Our histories from the effects of distortion, and to bring into conscious recognition the events in our lives that caused repression of spirit, fear, and emotional attachment. This, I suggest, is an underlying prayer for help buried deep in the heart of each individual.

We are answering our own prayers. This "Way", this "Quest for Healing" of ours is the answer to our own deeply buried prayers. It is the rescue of our inner child, and the retrieval of our own true souls.

On Compassion, Understanding and Help

By identifying the prevailing sentiment we may know the dominating energy of the moment. The dominating energy is always the unfulfilled one. It is the energy of desire and is the commanding energy. It is the demanding energy of the moment.

It is the energy that is speaking in the unseen and is always the voice, however inept, of the hidden prayer. This is why it is said that Allah knows the secrets of the innermost heart.

If the voice is negative, and projecting in the form of hatred, anger or resentment, then it is the product of (the) frustration (of desires).

Frustration is almost always the product of ignorance (as in inability), or distraction (as in lack of focus).

In other words, a lack of understanding.

Understanding is the goal of the quest. Understanding is what transforms the desiring student into the desired Teacher in Us All.

How can it be offered if it is not attained? It cannot be feigned. If there are still desires in the heart for it then understanding is not yet achieved. Understanding is the help! It is the victory and the opening.

Real understanding begins with a compassionate interest and the knowledge that underneath every Dominating Energy (or act of frustration) there is a responsible cause that is fundamentally benevolent and healing in nature.

I call this the "Primary Understanding". If motivations and primary causes can be truly understood and personal dreams truly honored, then frustrations can be recognized as simple expressions of the challenges to be overcome. This can then take place in cheerful, matter-of-fact discussion.

The implementation of this approach can eliminate the need for the expression of anger and resentment, which are the concomitant reactive hostilities of pointing blame (at a person), or finding fault (with a situation).

If these hostilities are already out in the open, then it might be useful to observe that their true purpose is simply to bring focus and constructive attention to the perceived frustrations toward the goal of fulfilling the primary causes.

Questions arise with the suspicion that the underlying causes and motivations are not clearly understood and honored. (Are they then not honorable? Do they need modification or at least some validation and confirmation? The phrase "Reality Check"' springs to mind.)

Now the deep work begins and it requires yet another understanding - "why is it important?" This is what separates the men from the boys, so to speak. It is the secret of the phrase "one person at a time".

Tradition has it that if you save one human being, you've saved all of humanity and if you kill one human being, you've killed all of humanity.

We have the capability to Save with the right words and to destroy with wrong words.

A famous writer was asked how he would define his life .

He replied ' I have been a drug dealer all my life.I have been dealing in the strongest drugs known to mankind,WORDS'

If you save one heart you've saved all hearts, and if you break one heart you've broken all hearts. If the smallest act of charity (giving) is picking up a stone from a pathway, imagine the significance of bringing one heart to God.

The Arabic words for "charity in the form of help or assistance", comes from the same root as "confirmation", "validation", "truth", "truthfulness".

All stem from the same root: sadaqa (to confirm, to verify, to give - some derivatives are sidq, saddaqa, siddiq). Faqir (poor), means one in need (of help, charity).

The Qur'an states that charity (sadaqa) is for the fuqara`, the truthful poor. And what do we have to give? Just giving. Going out in search is giving. Offering help is giving.

I will emphasise Again that Deep down, every person seeks understanding. Understanding can be felt as help and as the prerequisite to being helped, and all of us are needing and hoping in our heart of hearts to be helped.

This makes us fuqara`. Help is divine and from the Divine. What does this make the helper? Divine! That is the secret of Giving. Giving is from the Divine!

Receiving help is self-affirming and validating of life-efforts. In other words, it helps us to heal our hearts and prepares us to pass it along. Receiving help affirms our understanding and thereby our goals and sense of rightness.

We are all struggling for success. Having a really clear understanding of our true motivations and a compassion for the needs of humanity is a means of achieving success.

If we can know and manifest the truly benevolent nature of our own motivations, then we can help others to find theirs. So being understood is a prerequisite to being helped, and we all need help. This is the original ISLAMIC Way.

In order to be truly fulfilled we must be truly fulfilling. ", or, the fulfilled, pleased self and the fulfilling, pleasing self. The requirements for becoming a fulfilled and fulfilling human being.

This means (in the short form), give "unto you Lord His (due) rights, unto your family (humanity) their (due) rights, and unto yourself your (due) rights." These realities will approach when the sincerity of your devotion is confirmed.

The Dynamics of Sadaqah (Charity, Giving)

He also says that were he not to check the actions of some men by the actions of others that oppression would rule the earth.

By the same principle, were He not to make giving a requisite to receiving, there would be no good deed done on the planet at all.

Charity is blessed. Giving (for the right causes) attracts barakah (blessing). The proof of intention is action and action is a giving (contribution). The quality of the action (giving) can certainly vary, but you become what you do, and speech is also action.

TRUE FOLLOWERS OF ISLAM

Purification can take the form of learning the things that are required of you for congenial social interaction, studying Soul-manifestation for the purpose of self-application.

Concerning the word sadaqah, it is used in many ways. Allah says in The Qur'an that charity is for the poor, the traveler, the orphan and widow.

Secrets of the Divine

(revealing the distinction between the "enlightened" and the realized)

Every moment is a direct manifestation of Allah! People will either continue in the illusion that they are the doers or stop (and keep company) long enough to realize that they are not.

This is the difference between the realized and the unrealized, the knowing and the unknowing.

All knowledge has three stages, the hearing, the witnessing and the experience of the reality, or the deep knowing. The secret here is that it is only from the divine permission that real awareness is accomplished, and that permission can only be had by those who know its secret.

Allah causes science to behave in a predictable manner and the moon to follow the sun. He causes the outward sciences to behave in one manner and the inward sciences to be in a different form.

He causes the knowledges of creation to appear fixed for an appointed time, and allows for energy to move through them predictably and unpredictably in accordance with His will. He is the cause of the predictable events as well as the immediate.

Esoterics of Divine Permission ('Idhn)

Bismillahir-Rahmanir-Rahim. I begin with the name of Allah, whose mercy is such as to grant a person such as myself the possibility of a small insight into the workings of His mysteries, that such insight might be revealed and prove useful to seekers on the pathway to Him, the Almighty, the Wise, and the Glorious.

Islam as a way 'out' of the dangers of contemporary life, as a means of inward travel, and as a method of transforming the quality of life itself.

This is the least of the owned permissions, and is more than sufficient for the seekers of spiritual realities and for the salvation of their adherents.

It is also common that its use has trickled down from the lofty heights of high spiritual accomplishment into the mundane world to be used by the people of no true understanding.

The hallmark of these people is that they accept Divine favor upon themselves, but avoid the practices designed to lift them to the higher stations.

They love and are grateful for their own society, their company and their circles of remembrance, but are averse to accepting the way of the Prophet and thereby entering into the reality at whose door they are contented to sit.

Their 'idhn is from their mouths only, and has no relevance in realm of the true People of Allah.

Who are these people I am writing about?

On the Healing Power of Permission

It is said in a well-known tradition that prayer will avert the decree. Understand that surrender to the lower human nature is surrender to the decree, or "the way things are" and "the way things work".

This makes one completely susceptible to all of the apparent laws of "cause and effect that are part of the illusion, including the physics of health and diseases,

Chapter Six

Bismillah Life Coaching and Your Life

Fundamentally, the events in your life are governed by your beliefs.

Effort is prayer, so choose the direction of your efforts with wisdom. Moving in the direction of a healer is effort and prayer.

Moving in the direction of the Bismillah Life Coach is asking to learn about right and effective living. Realization, learning, study, practice and remembrance are efforts rewarded with Barakah, and Barakah heals.

A manifestation of this is the obvious benefit brought to humanity from communities and community effort.

Hadith has it that "the Hand of Allah is on the community". Individual effort to reach truth is rewarding to the community of that individual; one example being that a whole community need not study medicine if there is among them one devoted and successful student/practitioner.

Therefore, the more studious the hakim (healer, wise one, doctor, life coach) is of the essential realities of life, and the closer s/he draws to Allah (the Essential Oneness pervading all reality), the more power (permission) that Oneness grants to the Healer to pass on to the student or patient.

Call it EFFECTIVE education. The effect is that the student benefits from association with the practitioner by a manifest increase in health and understanding.

The nature of healing is that first the permission is granted, then the openings for the spirit of life are made by the elimination (by removal or penetration) of the impedances.

When the spirit comes into contact with the soul, the soul becomes inspired to new life, which inspiration moves the body (i.e. brings the spirit of life to the body).

Even the most inexperienced student of True Faith in the Divine Power of One God can be instrumental in the most wonderful healing miracles by inviting the friends to share in the benefits of the Divine circle and meet with the Truthful teacher/truth seeker.

Some Teachers do know the nature of ultimate health, and can manifest/ transmit the benefits of that knowledge, by means of which the astute student may also come to know the nature of its Origin.

True teachers have always been blessed with the key to healing.

It is called 'meaning and implying - to face with intent or intention, to pay attention to or send energy (or love) towards.

It is noted in many treatises that this power was exclusive to the inspired Truly Faithful Teachers and their empowered representatives and there was no mystery that it was a dispensation from the Divine.

Blessings upon the present. So be Present, if you want the blessings of Presence.

On the value of proper Guidance

ALL healing is done directly by Allah who needs no permission to do anything He chooses nor does He need any facilitator.

However, in most cases, right guidance is required in order to recieve gratitude and reform habits. It is often times difficult to heal if there is no proper arena for regeneration and gratitude.

Such an arena also serves as a means of preventing arrogance and falling again into the habits that caused the illness of Weak Faith in the first place.

The power to heal is strengthened when there is an avenue of guidance and reparation for the client.

That's why healing is such a famous part of the Islamic heritage. Permission to heal is given concomitant to the acceptance of a proper life style.

The power of permission to heal ('Idhn) often equates equal to the level of guidance held by the guide, and the level of guidance held by the guide equates to his station in the unseen.

Contemplate the value of proper guidance. Health is maintained. Gratitude is expressed because it can be received and channeled properly.

Lessons are truly learned and put into proper context. All sorts of benefits are derived. The client becomes a healer in the least case by witnessing to the 'power' of the healer and sharing the experience with others, all of which goes to the increase of the glorification of Allah, which is the Divine purpose.

In other words healing serves the divine purpose of spreading the knowledge of God exactly the same as disease is the result of ignorance of this divine knowledge.

The Healing Power of Intention

The Nature of Intention

Intention is the essence and the purpose of will, and <u>will is the first power.</u> - the Compeller, Who maintains creation by His Will alone.

It is the power of Divine Intention. Intention is the emanate force behind the power of Divine Compelling that manifests, supports, and maintains existence. <u>"Allah was alone and wished to be recognized, so He created."</u>

Will is the Essence of deed, act, action, accomplishment, creation, and healing. Will, the act and the power, is solely from The Divine.

It is said in The Qur'an "They will and Allah (the Divine) wills. And yet you cannot will except it be the Will of Allah.

"This ayat is used to describe the ingratitude of the selfish who use the divine gift of will for ultimately damaging ends.

Intention is the key to the power and efficacy of will and that may be the answer to the question of why we are so feeble in our accomplishment of that which we intend.

Why is our healing power so weak when we think of our intention as so strong? Is it that our intentions are not pure enough to attract sufficient Barakah for their successful accomplishment?

If Barakah (blessing) is the substance of Creation, let's look at the word 'creation' in two ways.

The most obvious is the noun denoting all Manifestation of the Essence of Allah, and another denotes the constructive endeavors of humanity.

Again, if Barakah is the substance of creation, and intention is that which attracts Barakah, then does it not stand to reason that intention is the criterion of successful endeavor?

People create in reality! They are not mere metaphor the verses of The Qur'an in which it is stated that we are building our homes in eternity.

By understanding the nature of Barakah we can, Insha'llah, draw people to it and thereby empower them, by means of education in proper intention, with sufficient Barakah to accomplish their life's work.

In general all work is healing; either in this world or in the next, either for self or for others.

If the intention is aimed at healing a greedy wallet then it needs an inordinate amount of amassed physical power to overcome the resistances of the universe .

The results, because of their unpraiseworthy intention and thereby natural tendency to defy edification must necessarily be doomed to the realm of the merely temporary.

Intention is a result of what's in our hearts. Intention is a full half of accomplishment. Tradition states that we are REWARDED (with success?) ACCORDING TO OUR INTENTIONS, and judged by what's in our hearts, so let's discover the ultimate in perfectly pure intention, and purify of our hearts and souls from all illusion, ie. other than absolute Universal Goodness, Love, Truth and Realization.

Doesn't the process of forming an intention consist of casting an image and exploring the possibility of it's coming true? Isn't this process of 'searching for the right course of action' actually the process of mentally casting images in search of the blessing, a green light from above, a sign of (at least potential) success?

Suppose the Real Success is to be found in a course of action that lies outside of our limited body of knowledge.

How can we consciously heal ourselves without first allowing space for the possibility (i.e. giving ourselves permission)?

How can we be really well (experience real health) without first knowing what it is and what to do with it? What is it that keeps us ill at ease or dis-eased?

Surely it's ignorance. Is it possible that we cannot imagine what it is like to be really well? Who benefits from our ignorance? (Now that's a loaded question.)

Have we really reached the end of our rope? What does that mean? Could it be that we can no longer envision further usefulness for life? Could it be that we have fulfilled OUR LIMITED INTENTION and cannot find anything else or better to do?

Why is it that the True Believers insist that the search for knowledge is incumbent from the cradle to the grave?

Life must have a purpose, and not necessarily a predetermined one, but one which may be discovered in the course of following it.

This brings us to the point of investigating the principle offered by Bismillah life coaching of "Purification of Intention".

Purification of Intention

Intention is most often motivated by desire, so it would seem that our strongest intentions would be guided by our innermost desires, and that the purpose of exploring active imagination is designed to bring out (express, come to terms with) innermost (and all) desires.

Intention can also be (and equally often is) motivated by knowledge.

It would seem that there are (at least) two ways to reach a conclusion concerning the realities of the 'inmost desire'.

One way is by exploration, the way of western psychology, and the other way is by the acceptance and study of 'Objective Truth', the Knowledges of which have been interjected into the human experience by Divine Will, or Revelation.

You are aware that the whole job of a true teaching servant of God is to deal with each person according to the level of their willingness to understand (Himmah).

Ego is threatened by the concept of 'objective truth' because it implies opposition to, limitation or annihilation of 'subjective truth', which is its (ego's) food and sustenance. Objective truth represents "Father's home!" to the happily mischievous and tyrannically unruly child of selfishness.

However, adherence to false knowledge and ego is that which prevents the positive influences of Truth.

Denial of the existence of objective truth or reality is a subjective choice the deliberate and misguided intention of which is to prevent and deter the benefits and influences of the benevolent life force, which is positive and purposeful in orientation, and healing and constructive by nature.

It is the suggestion throughout the general theme of these Words is that you be willing to deal with (investigate) the possibility of the existence of objective truth .

The possibility that it might be to your advantage to know how and why to form a firm intention to conform to and comply with the dictates resulting from your investigation.

From this you will surely find a whole new meaning to the words 'reality' and 'realization' and a whole new depth of meaning to your TRUTH studies. Now that's "Purification of Intention"'.

Intention in the view of the Truth Seeking

"The body has a single organ the health of which determines the health of the entire body, and that organ is the heart. " -- Imam 'Ali

There are (at least) two equally truthful meanings to this statement. The first is the outer, absolute literal meaning pertaining to physical health, but which in reality (Haqiqat) is still dependant upon the inner, esoteric spiritual meaning that true health (spiritual health) is totally dependant upon the heart's being free and clear of anything 'other' than Allah, Purity, Absolute Truth.

Cleansing the heart of all that is 'other' than Allah is the ultimate enlightenment. Self purification - Islamic purity) is the science by which, with the Permission of and by only the Will of Allah, the heart may be so cleansed.

The ultimate 'coup-de-grace' (Nirvana, Fana') is a gift from Allah Himself (what isn't), and cannot be 'attained', but it can and must be prepared for.

Such is the goal of the purest of intentions. ie. to become a TRUE SERVANT OF GOD, whose feet are solidly on earth and whose heart is wholly and certifiably in heaven.

Purity of Intention (Ikhlas un-niyyat) and willingness to maintain it (Himmah) are the ultimate healing forces and Surrender to the Will of the Divine (Islam) is the ultimate means of fulfilling that intention.

If you have no intention to fulfill your intention, then you have no intention. Hence the popular phrase "No Islam, NO INTENTION."

The Flavor of Surrender

TRUE ORIGINAL ISLAM is such a perfect way. The knowing of surrender is so easy when understood properly.

It's reasonably simple.

Surrender is the source of harmony, and contention is the root of discord. When one is in contention, one is not in surrender.

If you are in contention with your self (which is the case for almost everyone), you are probably in need of help or stuck forever.

However if you are fortunate enough to find yourself in contention with a Bismillah Life Coach, then the problem is resolved by simple surrender.

The nature of the `idhn (divine permission) of the TRUE BELIEVER/ SERVANT is that it is not to be argued with. It is an absolute authority, not based on the correctness of opinion, and completely independent of your approval.

If you are beloved, you will not be argued with, but simply forced, by love, into surrender.

Surrender implies the attainment of harmony (happiness) through the release of contention, not through the winning of argument.

The point is always your surrender (happiness) and eventual ability to recognize the difference between its presence and its absence.

In surrender, nothing needs to be proven. All things flow easily and naturally. The flavor of surrender to a True Believer is the flavor of surrender to The Divine.

When you are at peace with a True Believer you are at peace with Allah(GOD ALMIGHTY).
When you are not, you are not.

Surrender brings peace of mind.
Peace of mind allows the heart to open.
An open heart unveils the Field of Beauty.
and in the Field of Beauty the deep being is free.
The love of the deep being is its solitude with Allah.
And it welcomes only the company of other deep beings.

Alone but not alone, the deep being is identified by its love.

When the need is lost, and the field of the heart discovered,
all the concepts of the imagination disappear,
and there is only that field of truth to be enjoyed.
In the field of truth the deep being emerges,
and it is the deep being who is the true owner of the body.
The deep self is content to abide in the field of truth.
It is the true owner of the body, which is often captured by the mind
and its susceptibility to the illusions of ego,
the divisive self, the sensor of relationship,
the responder to desires and reactive defenses.

It is in the surroundings of peace that the student who is willing to give
up everything will have the opportunity to discover this true being, the
truth of their reality, allowing it to emerge.

The Invitation

The best of those are the ones who do Good Deeds and invite others to
do the same.

In Islam, self-education is praised and encouraged, for it is the
manifestation of true desire and sincere intention, and will result in the
best of accomplishments.

At a very young age I realized that I had to learn and open my understanding
of the human thinking and go back to the Original Islamic foundations
of muslims being the healers for humanity, there to serve all mankind.

The biggest mysteries were in people, especially my muslim brothers and
sisters.

I could not understand why the muslims were not keen on sharing the
good fortune that God Almighty had Gifted them,Islam.

Surely if you are gifted a nice braclet/aftershave/perfume, a nice car(if you are that lucky)you will want to share your great gift with people you associate with ie:friends, family, work friends(even if it is just to make them envious of you.

Being un- Faithful and un- grateful to the Gift -Giver is frowned upon in any society in the World, afterall how many situations have you known in your life where strong relationships have been cut to pieces,Because the Gift reciever has not been seen to be Grateful or has not been seen to appreciate the Gift.

You Fail to Appreciate the TRUE VALUE OF YOUR GIFT OF LIFE><FAITH><LOVE><THE SOUL><THE MIND><THE WONDERS OF NATURE ><THE VALUE OF TIME

My years of extensive study, research and self-education in Islam, Soul studies, Natural and Energy Healing, Homeopathic Medicine and Oriental Philosophy have always been for the sole purpose of helping me to deepen my understanding of Self, spiritual and human psychology.

The point has always been self-improvement - to become a deeper human being, more in touch with my True self, a better counselor, through an understanding of the spiritual nature of psychological problems, a better healer, showing, in the way of transformational psychology, the 'flip-side' of emotional and physical difficulties, and a better therapist, offering healing and therapeutics to ease the sufferings of the mind.

In short, a life coach and healer. The principles and results of these studies, along with many others, will be outlined in detail in this and many others works in progress.

In my early college years, I was moved to feel that the way of formal education was not for me, and that I would prefer a life of direct experience, whatever it might lead to, over a life of learning, without experience, what others would have us learn.

After some time in the School system and some years of amazing adventure and travel, spiritual search, study, I understand that a classical education, in Islamic or any other spiritual study, is much more rigorous that a few years spent in a modern college or university especially if you are a Curious Maverick.

It required a lifelong dedication to the learning of the path of the Truly Faithful Muslim.

In the Classical Islamic Tradition, certification, for the believers, comes with a "Permission" to teach, a formally applied for and patiently earned authorization, a "nod" of recognition that the subject matter is now understood, from a currently established and recognized Life Coach in the field.

This form of education is not for everybody, nor am I recommending it as such.

The benefits that an individual, a group or a society can reap from accepting and recognizing the presence of one educated in this manner are great. It is the basis of the spiritual communities of old.

It is not to be thought that spiritual realization is in some manner 'impractical', unworthy of a 'real achiever', or frivolous and 'off the point'.

It is becoming increasingly obvious that it is the point.

The whole point of peace is to be able to self-realize. Even play and love are opportunities to realize the true value of self. But without peace, there is little opportunity to enjoy, and without enjoyment, there is no self-realization.

The disruption of peace is the manifest purpose and energy of the shaytan (referred to in religious studies as Satan, or the great distracter) and the point of war.

The war and turmoil of the mind caused by subliminale messaging with no peace in sight.

STOP-non meditation Break

Stop!Close your eyes.Breath in deeply,Slow everything down .

As you slow everything down you start to feel the things we take for granted.

You feel Allah's presence in everything.

Evil in all it's guises would like you to keep speeding along.

God would like you to slow down and just think, feel,Appreciate(even if that means you comparing your life to someone else who may not be as fortunate in worldly gains but spiritualy richer)all the gifts we as humans do not give ourselves time to appreciate.

Achieve all in Life with GOD-REALIZATION as your Highest GOAL.

It is to keep us distracted by and involved in our fears, whatever they may be, for All our lives, that we will never have the opportunity to self-realize, to know and honor God, and attain truly successful and magnanimous lives.

The purpose of struggle is to end struggle. But we do not end it by domination, for that would entail the further struggle of constant vigilance against an unseen enemy, and this is the very situation the World society finds itself in right now.

We end struggle by giving up struggle, by surrendering our lives to God (Allah) in a New World and "taking our chance". If Allah wills, and He does, that we have long, healthy and prosperous lives, then nothing can prevent that from happening, in a peaceful, easy and natural way. And if He does not, then nothing we do can make it happen.

This is not to imply that the goal of Surrender is a long, peaceful and prosperous life. It is not. That is an expected byproduct, an endless overflowing of bounty upon us from the One who created life to be rich and rewarding.

The true goal of Surrender is simply to Know God, in this and every moment, and to rejoice, to be happy and manifest in that endless moment and knowing.

Now back to therapeutics and healing. It is understood in the Original islamic way that when one truly knows oneself, one knows "all things" in the sense of that which is pertinent to Self and God-realization.

This is not a knowing as in stored information, which is obviously, and dangerously, limited and limiting.

It is a true knowing of Source - which knowing is the source of knowing, knowledge and understanding.

This may or may not be easily grasped by the analytical mind - and that's why it's referred to by many analytical minds as "mystical". But it is a well-known fact among Bismillah life coaches, spiritualists and spiritual healers of all ways and faiths, and is, in Islamic psychology, considered to be the requisite groundwork for True health and Success, without which nothing of any great consequence will happen. And this is proving itself true in All society Negating This.

In the end it is only that connection to Source-personal that can be discovered, established, strengthened and confirmed in a United World.

Any way, path or religion may be offered in the form of an opening to continue walking in the way of the Realized, the way of the true Muslim (Surrendered to God) and the way of the Truth seeker.

One of the Biggest Challenges to overcome will be Hypocrisy in all it's different Guises.

Allah is your real Salvation and your ultimate Life is being in a state of GOD-REALIZATION with True love of all of Creation-Just look around you and you will see everything As it is for Real- A Miracle in motion.

The word Muslim then holds a different Attention from the World as a True Healer of civilized Society irrespective of where on this planet You Are.We can Help everyone To Realize their True calling.

Accepting that is your choice, and it should be looked at only after the healing, the peace, the fulfillment, the self-contentment and the satisfaction is found in the way of realizing God, Self and Unity.

This recognition is the Truth, the true wisdom of honor and recognition. It is the highest goal in a Truth seeker and Islam. Seeking it and passing it on is the true way of healing the heart in the classical original Islamic tradition.

A TRUE BELIEVER'S KNOWLEDGE OF GOD

The True Believer's/Truth seeker's/The Faithful's way to knowledge of God is the fastest way imaginable. It is more than instantaneous, because you knew it already.

Our job, as life coaches is simply to remind you that it is there, show you how to feel it, teach you how to remember it, and how to show and remind others.

Knowledge of God is instant healing, for you know from inside yourself that God creates only for His Truth to be known. He did not create except to show Himself, and to be loved and appreciated for His glory, love and mercy.

There is no limit to the praises of God. He is endlessly manifest in ourselves and on the horizons.

He it is who has sent down unto mankind His revelations and scriptures both old and new. These revelations take on many forms and are shown by Truth teachers, True seekers, True Believers and the Truly inspired.

The light of the sun of truth lands upon the hearts of mankind like a huge meteor from outer space landing on the surface of the earth, colliding, exploding, and dispersing itself everywhere.

It is to be felt and interpreted as each heart will, and done with as each mind chooses.

Always, within Every age, there are those who will look for the source of this knowledge. Where did it come from? How did it get here?Questions Most Need Answers To Only A Few seek to gather in this dispersion of religious and spiritual knowledge and return with it to its source.

Among such people are the Teachers, in quest of knowledge from the cradle to the grave.

The original Islamic message to you, oh beloved of God, is to search about the way to know God from within yourself.

Look for the teacher who heals your heart, in whose presence your heart feels at peace, and sit with that teacher and learn. The teacher and student in us ALL.

For a knowledge of God is truth for your mind, and the truth in your mind will bring you to recognize the goodness, love and kindness of your immortal being, and with that recognition comes a knowing of who you really are.

With a deeper knowing of who you really are comes a healing to your spirit, and with the healing to your spirit comes the energy for your heart.

With The energy for your heart comes the strength and feeling to your body, and with the strength and feeling in your body is your power to be well, to heal, to be healed, and to know the nature of God's grace upon you.

To know that you are well is what God wishes for you. For when you remember God, He remembers you. And surely it is in the remembrance of God that the hearts find peace, and with the peace comes the strength to know him, and to know that all is well, and to be Well.

So please know, accept and be grateful for the fact of life, that life is itself God's blessing and peace, and that it is, in fact, upon you.

Adopt

The Attitude of Gratitude in the morning and at night.

AN INTRODUCTION TO TRUE ORIGINAL ISLAMIC HEALING

True healing in the Islamic way is based on a knowing that at the core of each human heart there is only Divinity, which will always manifest as innocence, purity and love.

Through an understanding of the Divine Nature of health and the energetics of disease and emotional disturbance, a Bismillah life coach can offer effective means to dissolve personal problems on the physical and emotional levels.

Bismillah life coaching/healing also provides an accepted and rewarding path for personal support and spiritual development to guarantee the continued progress of its students.

The point of most spiritual practices and healing techniques is the release of your Divine Awareness and physical Love from the clutches of emotional bondage.

When the body is completely released, the soul becomes free to explore the treasures of the Divine. And that's where the real happiness of life begins.

The desire to experience truth is buried deeply within our hearts. Bismillah life coaching begins with a compassionate understanding that underneath every dominating energy (act of frustration) there is a truer motivation based on innocence and a responsible cause that is truthful, benevolent and healing in nature.

Divine awareness is release from emotional bondage. Emotional bondage is the root cause of fear, resistance, reluctance, hesitation, skepticism and all things that keep us from realizing the fullness and the Divinity of our lives.

Emotional bondage is what impedes the body from knowing the complete joy and happiness of Divine Surrender.

With the help of an experienced Life coach and healer, the sources and roots of these emotional bonds can be identified and their power over us neutralized.

The result is always increased freedom of movement, joy and hope for the future.

Bisimillah life coaching and healing offers an ideal arena for such self-investigation. In the safety of a trusted and guided friendship we may come to know and directly experience the loving truth in the secrets of our hearts.

Once we begin to know and trust the truly benevolent nature of our own true beings, we will be able to help others to find theirs.

Bismillah life coaching and healing offers not only the opportunity to know your self and become free but also to become active in the healing process of others and hence, the World.

All the Prophets and Sages insisted that saving the life of one person is equal to saving the whole world. And so it is with healing ourselves.

"Surely in the Remembrance of the Divine do the Hearts find Satisfaction." (The Qur'an)

Chapter Seven

The Powers of Bismillah and Your Health

A PEACEFUL HEART IS THE BASIS OF A HEALTHY BODY.

"Surely, in the Remembrance of the Divine do Hearts find Peace." (The Qur`an)

"So why are we so afraid of ourselves?"

"Simply because nobody will take the first step."

In the True way, spiritual maturity and presence (conscious, aware soul-inhabitation) are considered to be the requisites for true success.

The challenge then becomes to recognize and free ourselves from the residing influence of our history of fabricating fanciful and alluring illusions, and to trust, honor and speak from a truth that is inarguably our own, and from the very essence of our souls.

The magnetic attraction of this quality of authentic realization is that which stimulates trust, engenders confidence, and increases prosperity.

Healing the Body through Healing the Heart -

The Heart/Body Relationship

The body is a manifestation of the heart. It will and does follow the heart. Heal your heart and your body will (gratefully) follow. Guaranteed! This is the heart/body relationship.

Science has discovered that the Heart has a mind of it's Own.

Most of the essential discoveries in history have been denied, covered up or just plainly ignored.

The QURAN has within it's pages facts that have been proven over time but have never been credited or appreciated to Source.

Life on earth first came from water.

All living things come in pairs.

The cycle of Moon and Earth.

The existence of other worlds.

The Earth is Round Not flat.

That all existence is connected by the Author of All existence and that the most coveted prize for all creation is GOD-REALIZATION.

The heart is the battleground and coveted prize in the ongoing struggle between the (fearful) self-concept (ego), And the (trusting) true being (self, soul).

This struggle is the basis of conflict and the source of indecision, which manifests as physical discomfort. Incorrectly recognized, this physical discomfort becomes misinterpreted as disease.

It is then further mistreated until the body is weakened, overpowering the heart, and death by "natural causes" ensues.

A peaceful heart is the basis of a healthy body. Your heart is either at peace, or it is not.

Most of us are lost and floating downstream in the Great River called Denial. Denial (of feelings and self) is a societal strategy.

It's how we "get along" with each other. But it's also the basis of dysfunction, and spiritual suicide is no longer acceptable.

Upon seeking proper reflection, the heart can find its way out of denial into self-forgiveness and self-acceptance, and the physical manifestations of self-punishment and self-rejection will disappear.

Health, happiness and prosperity are immediate. Results are always available.

The Tradition of Spiritual Healing in Islam

"Healing the Body through Healing the Heart" is the fastest and most efficacious means of healing physical and emotional difficulty. It is the Essence of all True Healing, and I would like to show you how it works. I offer affordable sessions in reflection and confirmation of soul recognition, personal worth, true surrender, and inner connection. Please contact me through my email and through My website.Details later.

I call it (Life) Awareness Release Training (A.R.T.) The A.R.T. of Personal Success, or, the Way of Enlightenment and Health through Self-Recognition.

Awareness release is self-discovery. Training in it is the process of life. It can be catalyzed or accelerated by meetings with them who have acquired it.

This is the very essence of healing and is of immediate usefulness to people who feel that they need to discover, establish, enhance or confirm their personal connection with life.

Successful communities, businesses and relationships are built by successful people. God WANTS us to know prosperity and to be successful, individually, inwardly and outwardly. He expects it of us.

Personal Success comes with Surrender, Recognition and Connection. Resistance is futile. It's harder work to avoid this success than it is to accept it.

That's why everyone feels so burdened, because they're working in conflict against themselves. This is not Unity. And that's the point of enlightenment through self-acceptance – it truly lightens your burden.

Personal Success is a gift from God. There is nothing to do but learn to accept it. A.R.T. is the ART of eliminating resistance and becoming aware of your true personal power.

Surrender is the source of harmony, and contention is the root of discord. When one is in contention, one is not in Surrender. If you are in contention with your self (which is the case for almost everyone), you are probably in need of help or stuck forever.

The nature of the 'idhn (Divine Permission) of the True Believer is such that it is not to be argued with. It is an absolute authority, not based on the correctness of opinion, and completely independent of your approval.

If you are beloved, you will not be argued with, but simply forced, by love, into Surrender.

Surrender implies the attainment of harmony (happiness) through the release of contention, not through the winning of argument. The point of the master is never who's right. The point is always your Surrender (happiness) and eventual ability to recognize the difference between its presence and its absence.

Surrender brings peace of mind.
Peace of mind allows the heart to open.
An open heart unveils the Field of Beauty.
and in the Field of Beauty the deep being is free.
The love of the deep being is its solitude with Allah.
And it welcomes only the company of other deep beings.
Alone but not alone, the deep being is identified by its love.

When the need is lost, and the field of the heart discovered,
all the concepts of the imagination disappear,
and there is only the field of truth to be enjoyed.
In the field of truth the deep being emerges,
and it is to the deep being that the body truly surrenders.

The deep self is content to abide in the field of truth.
It is the true owner of the body, which is often captured by the mind
and its susceptibility to the illusions of ego,
the divisive self, the sensor of relationship,
the responder to desires and reactive defenses.

It is in the surroundings of peace that the student who is willing to give up everything will have the opportunity to discover this true being, the truth of their reality, allowing it to emerge.

FUNDAMENTALS OF HEALTH

GOD, FORCE, WATER, FOOD AND ENERGY

GOD

God is immediately available. There's one thing we have to do in order to avail ourselves of His full power for healing, and that is recognize our blocks to His energy of Love and clear ourselves from them. If we are willing to do that, then we can be healed even more quickly than normal or anticipated.

This clearing can rarely be done alone. For the very blocks that we carry are results of conscious decisions made under stress and they are now more difficult to detect.

For this reason we have "friends in high places", so to speak, who have sought the help and done the work and are more able to help us. All that is asked of us is that we consult with people of knowledge.

Bismillah Life Coaching

FORCE

The Force of the natural healing energy is always available and quite persistent. It is consistent with the love that your soul has for you.

Always there, always ready, always waiting patiently for you to return and come home.

It is present as the foundation of the very nature of creation. Nature, left alone, heals. The time it takes depends upon the surrender of the individual in need.

Good healers will explain the value and show the fastest way to this surrender, and often in only one session. So let the Force be with you. And the active word is "let".

Let Bismillah Life Coaching Release The Healing Forces within YOURSELVES

WATER

Water is the carrier of nutrients and waste. It also is able to convey energetic impulses rapidly, and to change its configuration according to the subtle energies of thought. Therefore, it is the original "shape-shifter".

The more pure water we have in out system, the cleaner and more easily our system will run. It will also respond more easily to our thoughts, and that's why prayers and thoughts turned to God for help have such a readily available influence.

Proper orientation of thoughts, recognition and resolution of blocks to healing (and there are, strangely enough, quite a few), receptiveness of the physical body to subtle energy shifts by maintaining proper hydration, and studied sensible nutrition, are the keys to rapid healing.

FOOD

The fundamentals of nutrition and natural dietetics should be learned from the simple and easily understood . There are many books and teachers of this way of understanding, but to date none have matched the master for simplicity and ease of explanation.

Grasping this philosophy is the simplest and easiest way to understand the fundamentals of the forces of nature and their influence on diet and health.

So try to find it in the original Islamic Teachings.

It is stated that The Prophet (peace be upon his Name Forever) said that one third of any meal should consist of water, one third empty and one third food.

One glass of water with lemon juice drank one hour before a meal is one of the best ways to sustain a healthy weight.

Exercise and positive attitude are even more important to sustain a healthy life.

ENERGY

By Energy I mean the daily influences on your life. It is essential for the passionate student to take a course in the basics of energetic and emotional healing which I will be offering shortly.

Probably after the publishing of This Book by the wonderful people at Lulu publishing Who I would like to thank.

They have shown real support from speaking to Logan in Sales to Stephanie,My project co-ordinator with Great Helpful advice with sincerety from ALL aswell as the Editorial Department.

May GOD bless you and make ALL your Journeys full of Love .

They have been Great along this journey of mine which has took nearly five years.

I do need a break as It has been a very emotional and spiritual quest which I have enjoyed.

I have Found my myself along the way.

Energy has a profound influence on us and it is possible to learn about it in such a way that the flow of benevolence, your "Power to Receive", is not interrupted.

ELEMENTS OF SOUL HEALING

The Basics of the Science of Transformational Psychology
Understanding the Nature of True and False Responsibility
as a means of Accomplishment

PART 1.

The Fundamental Technique of Transformational Psychology is
RECOGNIZING YOUR PERSONAL REVOLUTION
for in it is the Secret of

How your Lovingly Rebellious Soul is trying to Heal you in Spite of Yourself.

So stop TRYING to be good, and BE - fearlessly - who you really are.

"Take care of yourself" means to Recognize and Honor the Requirements of your Soul.

"Who recognizes (realizes, honors, knows) his True Self (Soul), recognizes (realizes, honors, knows) his Lord".

This is why The True Surrender (Al-Islam) to Rabbil 'Alameen (Allah) will release, with truth and love, the hold that the ego (the artificial, fearful and demanding conceptual self) exercises.

This allows the real Self, which is from Allah (the Essence) and returns to the Essence, to be our true guide, or Rabb.

Anxiety is at the root of every major or minor illness.

Peace is the only basis for Healing.

Relieve Anxiety and you've established Peace.

Nothing relieves anxiety like Success.

A Solid and Confirmed Inner Connection is the key to every Success.

Surrender to the Divine results in a Solid and Confirmed Inner Connection and brings Immediate Success.

Healing is therefore a matter of giving yourself permission to choose Surrender.

Relieving anxiety is a matter of recognizing its source.

Anxiety is a consequential manifestation of a choice - an accepting of false responsibility.

Having accepted false responsibility for true responsibility is the source of inner hypocrisy and conflicted belief structures.

Anxiety is the result of an imperfect Knowing of God.

Illness is a result of this inner duplicity. It is not our fault, simply the consequence of choices we've made.

We are free to make new choices. "Repent" in Latin means to rethink, in Arabic to return.

Accepting responsibility for choices made is the key to empowerment (to change).

Unity heals. There is a Perfect Knowing - it is the Goal of the Quest. God IS Knowable, Immediately.

Knowledge of Unity is the basis of knowing and understanding the nature of Perfect Health.

Self-esteem is based upon your estimation, and therefore knowledge, of God.

Your estimation/opinion of God (and self) will increase by keeping company with the True Muslims. This is why The True Muslim will offer Company and Availability, and explains the phenomenon of "Miracle Healing" that often takes place in their presence, through true faith.

The "Work" is the elimination of doubt and hypocrisy - resolving duplicity with Unity.

"Concern for provision is the first step of Denial."

(Prophetic Tradition).

1. Anxiety is the cause of every major or minor illness.

    Anxiety expresses itself as fear of the unknown, concern for provision or concern for the future. The job of anxiety is to keep you off balance and eternally distracted from giving yourself permission to know, and to be well.

    The sense is that if you are not anxious, or "ill-at-ease", you are somehow being irresponsible. It has become socially obligatory to be anxious and fearful for the future. The Prophet said that the world (our selves) was divided into two states (countries, camps, or lands).

    They are the "Dar us-Salam", the State of Security (Surrender, peace, trust and healing), and the "Dar ul-Harb", the State of Anxiety (suspicion, dis-ease, conflict and war).

2. Peace is the only basis for Healing. Relieve Anxiety and you've established Peace.

    Everyone wants his or her anxieties relieved. True Hospitality is the relief of anxiety. So everyone needs hospitals (joking) - hospitality. Relieve anxiety and you've established Peace, which is the basis for happiness. Anxiety is the first and primary disrupter of the happy energies of Peace.

    Every one's house should have Hotel Facilities with a great restaurant.

facilitating Guests.Close friends and distant friendships would become closer with the concepts of hospitality.

There I go dreaming Again.Sorry where was I!

It shows up as self-concern or concern for provision, and as such is the first breach of the innocent trust and contemplative adoration (known as Surrender) of living in the garden of the heart with the world waiting patiently to serve you.

Infants don't have self-concern and are born completely trusting and adoring. This is why the Prophet Muhammad said that all children were born Muslims, meaning- in a state of surrender and peace- Islam.

This is why children must be 'taught' responsibility. But unfortunately the responsibilities that they are 'taught' are the responsibilities of obligation to anxiety (the great false god of self-concern), rather than the responsibility to love and trust The Divine (Allah).

3.   Nothing relieves anxiety like Success.

Just thinking about success relieves anxiety. Try it. Or maybe you have difficulty imagining it. Take a course in guided imagery or visualization. It will really help.

See details of courses available contact our website.

4.   A Solid and Confirmed Inner Connection is the key to every Success.

Just studying all that is being written on the subject should be enough to convince you of this one. Outward success without the inner Connection doesn't last and doesn't bring the Satisfaction because it is only in the remembrance of God that the Souls find true Satisfaction.

Satisfaction of the Soul is called fulfillment.

All the seminars and books on "making it" and "success" in this world are based on the work of "Self-Dis-Covery", where you are Dis-Covering your true Being, or Soul Work. And of all the available learning systems and healing methodologies out there, there is none faster or more tried, proven and complete than the way of the Truly Faithful Believer in the One True God.

5.   Surrender to the Divine, at the hand of a Bismillah Life Coach, leads to a Solid and Confirmed Inner Connection and brings Immediate Success.

Soul Purification is the English words coined for the Science revealed to the Prophet Muhammad and developed by Muslim students, psychologists and Teachers.

6.   Healing is a matter of giving yourself permission to choose Surrender.

But will you? You can choose to be well. You can enter into the state of Peace simply by choosing to do so. It's called Surrender, and I will be offering regular classes and healing sessions. Details will be sent to all who register to help you recognize and understand it. Divine permission is already in place.

All will be welcome and with the internet services increasing the capabilities of transmitting valuable Information at speed to Any where is just a Blessing from Allah.

There are Evil people in different guises out there WE have to be vigilant for each other and WE will work to find that LOVE for GOD ALMIGHTY will win everytime.

Permission to be well, live long and prosper is definitely granted by God, and again, if you need help believing that, please start attending my classes, Available online if you cannot travel to lovely ENGLAND to see Me.

You are most welcome to join me for a delightful Feast in Anglo-Pakistani Cuisine with A cup of Green Tea to finish the Dinner in Pakistani style.

I love All people, Especially the wonderful People who through out their Lives have been Close to GOD-REALIZATION but Never Realized until you sit down together to Talk.

The scene becomes very Emotional as TRUE LOVE IS RECOGNISED in All its different forms but all originating from The SOURCE of All GOOD.

ALLAH.

Even given you know that already, the deeper question is, can you, and will you, give yourself permission to accept the Divine Permission?

This is the crux of the problem. It is not ever as easy as it sounds, or you would be in perfect, fearless health. If you are not, I'm sure you will find, with a little investigation, the part of you that chooses not to, and mostly out of some sense of prior obligation.

You choose your anxieties, because you feel that your happiness is tied up in them. Alas, you have "responsibilities" (you say with a deep sigh and a mock heavy heart.). But look deeper and you'll find that you're proud of them, you derive some happiness and satisfaction from them.

You consider them "worth the sacrifice" (you martyr, you) They make you happy, and you manifest a child-like and innocent pride in your "responsibilities" through a sense of concern and anxiety.

This anxiety, then, becomes your underlying (and commonly accepted) excuse for not paying attention to your true concern, i.e. your self and your health. You 'put it off until later', using your 'responsibilities' as the rationale for martyrdom, 'self-sacrifice', recklessness, and even suicide.

7. Relieving anxiety is a matter of recognizing its source.

    A famous channel has said that, "the bypass is in the recognition of the complication". Books have been written trying to express this, but try to look deeply into the following explanation.

8. Anxiety is a consequential manifestation of a choice - an accepting a false responsibility.

    Anxiety is felt to be an obligation, but it is actually a reflection of someone else, a conditioned reflexive behavior pattern triggered by thoughts, mostly of 'love' for another. But from the soul's joyous viewpoint, it is an act (as in stage play).

    It is hypocrisy, pure and simple, and the result of a co-dependent relationship. It is caused by accepting false responsibility to, for and from – 'others'.

    It is duplicity - not your true self! So false responsibility is a responsibility not to, for, and from your true self.

    Yet you must take responsibility for doing this to yourself, for inflicting unnecessary and hypocritical pain and suffering upon yourself.

    This responsibility is the key to empowerment, and without it you cannot initiate change in your life. (When you are really happy, and can see the truth of this simple, yet profound statement, you will be able to understand, forgive and heal not only yourself and others, but the 'sins' of your ancestors for seven generations.)

9. We have all substituted false responsibility for true responsibility. This is the source of duplicity and causes a conflict of our belief systems.

We have all substituted the false responsibility to concern and anxiety for our true responsibility to a perfect knowing of God - to know the Reality, which sheds light on and dispels our illusion.

This is the reason for the Wisdom teaching that we are living in illusion. It's as though anxiety is the only way to accomplishment.

It is my premise that this is exactly the responsibility that we do not want to accept, and toward which our Soul is in revolt, for it is, in reality, taking responsibility for someone else who is probably, in some very real sense, actually doing the same thing.

So are you a healer or a patient? When it comes to health, you are either a healer (listening to your true self and healing both yourself and others) or a patient (listening to someone else, of a doctor or medical system).

You are either taking responsibility for your current condition and thereby enabling yourself to change it (by letting it improve), or you choose not to, continuing in 'victim' mode, allowing and insisting that the responsibility for your health and well-being be placed in the hands of some 'other'.

So how can we stabilize the beautiful healing energies that we have tasted or are so familiar with? Check anxiety! Investigate the source of obligation! Free yourself from the bonds of relationship! (Just for a moment). Are you happy? (Just testing.)

We have all been taught (by 'others' - needy parents, etc.) that innocence and lack of concern is being 'irresponsible' (which we never really believed).

As a result, we now accept as axiomatic our 'obligation' to 'act' responsibly, by showing concern and accepting 'our share of the responsibility' to an anxiety-ridden way of life. This obligation requires us to 'act' (what we do not feel) - to 'behave' (as expected - by 'others'). Acting is pretending, masquerading.

Masquerading is putting on a mask. It's a kind of compulsory (defensive) hypocrisy. We don't really believe it, but because we cannot express our true selves and beliefs adequately, either to ourselves or to others, we are forced to overlook, disregard, and ultimately disrespect our own beliefs, and accept what we are being told, as the 'truth'.

So we eventually end up believing in and conforming to the way of anxiety, and forgetting the Peace and Joy that we were born with to bring into the world. Gone! Buried! Dig it out later, maybe. Or not!

This kind of responsibility always becomes required of us before we have learned how to properly take responsibility for ourselves. How to keep your children at home to serve you and help you fulfill your needs?

Impose your obligations and belief structure upon them before their freedom is discovered. Impede them from learning the secret of self-responsibility.

Learn the secret of self-responsibility and all will be provided for you. If you no longer have concern for provision, you will not sell yourself and your labors on the market as someone else's slave - for "a crust of bread', as the saying goes. In other words, you become 'useless' (to 'others'). Hooray for you!

10. Anxiety is the result of an imperfect Knowing.

Anxiety for the future is a manifestation of an imperfect faith. "Concern for provision is the first step of Denial." Perfect faith instills prefect trust.

Anxiety is the absence of trust. It is a manifestation of not knowing, of incorrect understanding, of imperfect faith. It is a fear for the unknown, and unknowing is exactly that, a direct consequence of lack (absence) of Divine Knowledge.

As you can see, we've all been deliberately misled regarding the matters of true faith and healing. The truth is that if you really knew God you would have no worries, only joy and gratitude, and endless personal magnetism to acquire your desires.

The potrayal of GOD Almighty as an angry, fearful, insecure, jealous and vengeful God is to be honest is shameful, disgusting and cowardly, however They flower it up.

Shame on you all who practice these obscene and as has been proven over time Very Damaging, Dangerously Destructive practices of Evil disguised as good.

Sowing the seeds of mistrust, disharmony and disunity among all of Mankind thereby stopping Full ONE-GOD-REALIZATION to ever be implemented.

If ONE-GOD-REALIZATION was implemented fully You would then become a constructive and healing member of society, instead of feeling like a slave, living your life to benefit others, attempting to assuage your disappointment and depression by consoling yourself with the ephemeral and all too transitory pleasures of material acquisition, and justifying it as love. Obligation is compulsion, not love.

Alcoholism,Drugs (soft or hard), cigarretes, cigars, anxiety, sexual depravity,Cruelty of any description including emotional or physical, over-eating(to fill the emotional void of feeling unloved) leading to overweight thereby leading to strains on physical wellbeing and many other forms of Negative UNGODLY activities the human race takes for granted which are SUICIDAL at the end of the day.

Human beings All need to TAKE stock of their thinking and start taking responsibility For their Actions starting with GOD-REALIZATION at the Top of the Agenda.

Show True Respect to Your One true lord ALLAH Almighty.

This must be Took seriously otherwise we will LOSE.

11. Illness is a result of duplicity. It is not our fault, but we chose it.

12. Accepting our responsibility is the key to empowerment (to change).

13. Unity heals. There is Perfect Knowing - it is the Goal of the Quest. God IS Knowable, Immediately. Peace is the source and foundation of the healing energy. Peace is found in the energy balance between the 'positive' and the 'negative'.

14. Anxiety is the first disruption of peace, and the first manifestation of energy imbalance, or lack of trust. Lack of trust is the first sign of lack of correct faith, and lack of correct faith is healed (can be healed immediately by knowledge) by turning to God with certainty and seeking certain knowledge (as in objective, transcendent truth).

15. The deep inward certainty (certain knowledge, objective, transcendent truth) is the closely guarded treasure of the Bismillah Life Coach and knowledgeable Gnostics of Allah. And it is said that the forgetfulness of the knower is still more powerful than the remembrance of the seeker.

* Allah! *

16. All this, plus my personal experience, leads me to know and believe that faith, love and freedom go hand in hand, and that love, and peace, HEALS ALL.

Knowledge of Unity is the basis of knowing and understanding the nature of Perfect Health

Correct understanding comes from Perfect knowing, and Perfect Knowing is the basis and Essence of Perfect Health. True Knowledge and remembrance of the Divine Benevolence of God is the Essence of Perfect Health.

There is Godly Knowledge.Just Stop and Think logically.Forget what you have been taught up until this moment.

Let this be your moment to take charge of your Life and your Happiness.

Connect to the source.

We are making head way in that area with help from great publishers and Established GOD-REALIZED Brothers and sisters, some in quiet lives and some in Busy lives.

Great Souls who have been granted the permission by GOD ALMIGHTY to help BISMILLAH to Awaken,Enlighten and make aware All of creation of it's True destination.

Which is to Love and be Loved in return.

Like all things of quality, it must be sought. Godly Knowledge and the remembrance of the Divine Benevolence of God is the basis and Essence of Perfect Health. It is the exclusive focus of the Truly Faithful Believer in the One True God.

17. Self-esteem is based upon your estimation, and therefore knowledge, of God.

True Self-esteem is the dynamic magnetism that shows you everything, and brings all things to you effortlessly. It is based solely upon your estimation (or knowing) of God.

18. Your estimation/opinion of God will increase by keeping company with the Beloved Servants of ALLAH wherever They may be or whoever they may be(Whatever label they may have be given or have given themselves).

    Your search for Them will never be Fruitless and I am sure You will be compensated with a life of Love,Respect and Peace.

19. This is why BISMILLAH LIFE COACHING offer company and availability and explains the phenomenon of "Miracle Healing" that often takes place in their presence.

20. The "Work" is the elimination of Hypocrisy - resolving duplicity with Unity.

A SUPERIOR MEANS

It's commonly thought that, since spirituality and life are separate, spirituality has no place in life, and especially in the doing of business.

It is also falsely assumed that since life is a matter of economic survival, the most practical (and lucrative) approach would be that which is farthest away from the essence, or truth. Hence develops the glib double-dealer, whose stock-in-trade is suave and convincing duplicity – the art of the gentle lie, so to speak.

Yet if you look in the business development section of your local bookstore, you will find that the trend in business and of the truly successful is everyday leaning more toward the realization of truth and reality.

It just makes good sense. The taxing toll it takes to maintain pretense and lies is causing the rapid erosion of human personal energy.

It is taking us farther away from our proposed goal of success rather than bringing us to it as we had hoped it would.

This all has to do with the shift from industry to information, and now to the need for a deeper, an absolute, if you will, truth by which to evaluate. It has, in the end, to do with our personal concepts of success and the goals we set to attain it, the motivations behind it, and the means we use to achieve it.

How many books are written by the rich or So called Successful extolling their concept of success, how they attained it, and how you can too? I read them in search of a definition of success that feels right to me, and I find nothing. I'm left with the deep feeling that I do NOT want to do what it is they recommend. Even stronger – I WILL not.

What, then, I ask myself, will I do? And among the myriad options that appear the one of "Nothing, absolutely Nothing!" feels without doubt, the very best choice. Actually, let me reword that. It feels to me to be the wisest (as in the absolutely smartest), the Superior choice - not "running away" from the false or artificially imposed responsibilities of my own and society's creation, but running TO the Recognition of a Superior means of achievement.

To see in the old paradigm, spirituality as mere escapism misses the point altogether. The Truly courageous ones who break away from and leave the common pursuits in Quest of the Superior - new and groundbreaking ways to attain, with peace and inner truth, the goals of outward prosperity and security.

So give yourselves a break. Stop deceiving yourselves and lying to others. Hear, listen, and pay attention to the calling of your True self, the one that's really tired of pretense and would love to find a better way. Afford yourselves the hospitality that you need to give your hearts a rest and think it through. Listen to, and receive from, the quiet love of your souls.

That is how you can Know God. Listen to the love of your souls.

EXPRESSION - THE SECRET TO PERFECT HEALTH

ISLAMIC YOGA, SOUL AFFIRMATIONS AND POSITIVE VISUALIZATION/MEDITATION.

This book will be coming out somtime in 2018(God Willing)

Watch out for snippets that you can request through our emails and websites.

I will see how I progress and If I can I will offer Webinars offering help on line connected to the book,Perhaps You can give me helpful tips on what other stuff to put in the book to make it Interesting.

You know I love you guys too much to ever let you down.

Here is a Small snippet from the upcoming book:

THE SECRET TO HEALTH IS SOULFUL EXPRESSION

It seems that expression is always of one of two things or some interesting or confusing mixture of both. In an easy analysis it might be said that we are always expressing either what's right or what's wrong. We are manifesting satisfaction and pleasure or dissatisfaction and complaint. In order to heal, both must be accepted for what they are, and not only without judgment, but also without preference.

The question in healing is not so much the content of the expression as it is who is doing the talking and what is really being said.

It's just a matter of what means we use, or what way we take, to see through our illusions. Once that is accomplished, the incredible nature and beauty of God is again visible.

So getting over our illusions is one of the promptings of the soul. What matters, and what life seems to be all about, is testing the means of accomplishment we have been given to see if they are successful. And if they are not, choosing to seek a superior means.

On Body, Soul, Heart, Mind, and Self

Soul is fine, It's there, watching, guarding and caring, and prompting you to pay attention, like it or not. Heart is fine. As long as it is beating, it is open to and in the Love of God. Body is fine. Whatever it's condition, Surrender and Acceptance is the key to the receiving of the healing love. Mind is good. Concepts and beliefs are personal, simply arising in consciousness, and can be changed or let go at any moment, since there is in reality no stone for them to be etched upon.

On Seeing God in Everything and the Annihilation of Desires

Let all these things be as they are, for they are as they are, but what seems to keep "getting in the way" of the fullness of our Divine experience is this willful thing we call our "self".

It's our self that keeps asking for and seeking satisfaction. It is in fact, only desirous of the annihilation of its desires, and it's the expression of this desirousness that wants, yea needs, to be heard. It's not even so much that it wants to be heard as it wants to be ex-pressed, as in said, done, gone, annihilated, not there any longer, in a word, satisfied.

Ahhh, satisfaction. What I'm saying here is that the ultimate satisfaction is desirelessness.

In THE TRUE PATH, this desirousness (or the desire for desirelessness) is called '- often translated as 'longing' - and it is considered to be the only essential quality for true success.

It needs only to be recognized for what it is. This is what I refer to as the root, or "spiritual" motivation for all expressions. It is the search for annihilation. Again, one of the big negatives, we do not want to be here. It is the innate spiritual desire to be only with God and free of all illusion.

Understand this. Can you see here how the recognition and honoring of our true spiritual motivation, manifested and known to be an innate quality of the soul, will be of great assistance in your healing practice?

This is the spiritual psychology that allows you to see and understand the truth of all expressions for the transformation of sins and curses into blessings and guidance.

This seeking for annihilation, with desire as the motivation, this "asking for satisfaction" is the natural Quest, the 'Search for the Truth', the 'ultimate destination', often thought to occur only after death, but which in reality is only the death of painful desire.

This motivation is an essential quality, without which there would be no drama of life. It is that quality that is the true spiritual seeker within us All, naturally. If understood, superior means can be acquired, and a destructive path will be gratified and replaced with a constructive one.

With this recognition, problems can be reduced to a simple and very natural desire for satisfaction, which, when seen in the light of the Knowledge, is realized to be, and thereby transformed into, an expression of the quest for satisfaction itself, the actual annihilation of desire and/or dissatisfaction.

When seen in this light, the need for the expression of desire/dissatisfaction is understood, and truly 'heard'. Then the perceived necessity for dramatization, or 'acting them out' is diffused, so to speak. Nor is one left with the feeling that they have not been heard - that they have been asked to repress them 'selves' yet again.

This "asking for satisfaction" is then recognized as an expression of the quest for the 'Knowledge of God', for the actual Physical KNOWING, the Supreme Satisfaction, the 'Tasting of' and the 'BEING in' the Reality that God alone exists.

Now the satisfaction of desire becomes an entirely different matter. And that is why it is said that the True way is that very thing. In the True way our souls are truly recognized, our desires are truly expressed and satisfaction is truly achieved.

We want God to hear us asking for our own annihilation. We want to KNOW that He hears us asking for our own dissolution, that only He exist. Just knowing that He hears is the beginning of satisfaction, and it is said that the end is in the beginning.

For knowing about God, or talking to God, or asking God for anything is praising God by considering God (rightly) to be worthy of being asked and capable of helping. And it is stated in ORIGINAL ISLAMIC contemplation practices that "God hears the one who praises Him". So the way to be heard is to praise, and therein lies the secret to all the success programs that are based upon 'positive' thinking and feeling' (like NLP).(contact our website for details and information on GOD-REALIZATION NLP)

The Secret to Perfect Health

The Secret to Perfect Health is Perfect self-expression. Who knows better the needs of the heart, body, mind, soul and self of the human being than the one who created it. So who can show us a better way to a perfect life, and a better way to perfect self-expression, than Allah?

On Healing the Spirit

Spirit is what moves us, and attention is what moves spirit. Wherever we focus our attention, there moves our spirit also. Spirit is the fire that removes the blocks that let the energy flow. Moving/kindling the Spirit is the essence of all healing arts - Kiatsu, Shiatsu, Acupuncture, spirit healing, energy healing and healing (focusing concentrated Divine Loving Attention), to mention only a few.

To really feel and kindle our spirit we must concentrate it.

A small example. Feel the concentration of your spirit when you contemplate a fond pleasure. Skiing? Biking? Sex? A movie? Relaxing with a good book like the One you are Reading now.

Focusing our attention on the Divinity (Allah) is not an easy thing, since He is NOT what you think He is and therefore how can YOU focus your attention on Him.

Quite conceptual, to say the least, and not very experiential. Fortunately we have learned the technique of remembrance, which was revealed through all the Prophets and taught by generations of kind-hearted and sincere believers and seekers from All around the world.

Leaders of mankind who practiced Compassion for All of Creation linked to GOD-REALIZATION were very Blessed with ALLAH'S Love in all it's wonderful Forms.

There have been so many over time in different Situations in History who have sought to make people question themselves about Their true calling in their lives(whether they acknowledged it or not God was ONE to their souls as THE Eternal Source of True love) along with

Civil Rights Leaders From America,India,Africa and Many more wonderful Souls who have sacrificed so much for Humanity including in Most cases their worldly Lives.

Many acknowledge Their Thanks to God Almighty and their gratitude is shown in their sacrifice of Wealth,Time and compassion towards their fellow humans.

Love conquers Again.

We should all Remember their True Goals were Unity and God-realization Through Love.

Some True greats in Humanity have Not fully Realized That GOD-REALIZATION has been granted to themselves.

We only wish that they would Allow their Authentic Selves to Shine Brightly for they owe it to ALLAH Almighty, for He has given them much from his bounties.

Respect from among their fellow mankind being the Highest Goal for any human.

The goal of spirit is it's own annihilation in Divine Presence. It is the fabled Simurgh, the large-winged bird that arises from ashes to fly to the sun only to fall into ashes and arise again.

A concentration of spirit needs to be present in order for it to focus on and annihilate itself in Presence. Spirit is a burning flame that consumes itself and only Presence is left. Presence is what remains when all else is gone.

It's an easy thing to know God, since God is never not present, we need only to turn our thoughts there, and boom, there we are. That's why one of the qualities attributed to God is that of Al-Tawwab, the oft-returning acceptor of our Repentance and Rethinking.

After this "connection", or "re-charge", how quickly do we turn away? In a sense, we "use" God to regenerate our spirit and then turn our spirit away from God to use it for the fulfillment of our desires, as though He is not capable of fulfilling them better than we.

This is, in a sense, disrespectful and, in a sense, hurts God's feelings, because He wants to prove a point. He wants not only to fulfill our desires for us, and indeed He does, but He wants us to know Him, and know that He IS the fulfillment of our desires.

Feel the comparison between the lover and the beloved. See this in YOUR relationship. In your deep heart, do you not want to BE the fulfillment of your beloved's desires? Is that not the ultimate satisfaction? Do you not want his/her desires to be so oriented that you CAN be his/her fulfillment?

The formula is simple. BE your Beloved! For only the Beloved (Allah) IS, or can be, the fulfillment of all desire. That is His promise, and that is exactly what He wants to be and do. In order to do this, we need to KNOW that His Presence is with us at all times.

But what does this require of us? The focus of our spirit on Him and Him alone. Before we focus on "how" we can do that, let's look at a few areas of thought.

On the foolishness of chasing dreams

"But that will take me away from my life and my responsibilities and/or the accomplishment of my dreams and desires", you say?

What an intense amount of energy and frustration is spent on the chasing of dreams. Literally we waste our lives away in pursuit of an illusory "happiness" that is always just on the other side of an "if only". Yet we will all readily admit that a moment of deep contemplation upon the Divine Existence of God brings into our lives that very joy and happiness that we are "seeking/trying" to "establish" on a "permanent" basis in our lives. This is stated so nicely in The Qur'an "Verily it is in the remembrance of God that the hearts find their fulfillment".

How simple it is. Why are we seeking? Because we have not "found"! Why are we "trying"? Because we have not yet "succeeded". Why do we want it "established"? Because we have not yet discovered that it already is. And why do we want it "permanent"?

Because nothing less will satisfy. Don't you see that the "life of this (your, private, individual) world" is an exact mirror image of the Real World, into which God (Allah) wants you to step with full faith, trust and confidence?

So how do we get this faith, trust and confidence? Simple. Pick it up from them that got it. "And who are they", you ask? I put it to you, the walkers of the ORIGINAL ISLAMIC way. "And how can they be so sure", you ask? Well, ask them. Meet them. Read them. They've all tried it and to a person wish to be living testimonials that it is the truth. That is why "bearing witness", or testimonial to truth, is such a strong part of their lives.

"And where did they get this from?" They got it from the truth itself, from themselves, their observations, their own willingness to believe in, search and explore possibilities. They got it from others who had done the same and found it to be a safe and A well-trodden path.

They got it from seeing Love in desperation. And when they heard that this was, in truth, the very message with which all the Prophets were sent, they knew it was the truth already in their hearts, and believed the message of the Prophets. So they joined them and their communities to live in, enjoy and spread the word of this Way.

Kindling your spirit is the beginning. Ongoing life and living, in and by the Presence of the Divine, is the goal. . Taste the true joy of life, Drink the wine from the cup of love, and feel the peace of certainty and knowing.

Feel the existence of endless Divinity, living your life in peace, security, love, and friendship, with understanding and healing for yourself and others.

The Law of Positive Attraction will Find it's Rightful place in your life in Each moment of Your Life.

Above all, feel and know Divine Love.

On Religion and Spirituality

Religion without a spiritual quest is death. Just ask the people of religion. They're all waiting to die to know God. Meanwhile they know only what they know and are steadfast in their resolve to stick with it, Whether they are Christians,Muslims,Jews,Hindus,Budhists or the other thousands of Faiths.

All doing their bit but Not enough and All They need is a SHIFT in Focus to complete their missions and to put ONE GOD-REALIZATION as the FOUNTAIN to Nourish the garden of Peace,Happiness,Contentment, Love,Unity,Joy and above All Satisfaction knowing that you have Reached Your True Goal.

Even though their Original religions insist that the quality of a true believer is that of a seeker of knowledge from the cradle to the grave.

Ask the people without religion. For the most part, they want nothing to do with it, and for the very same reason. On the other hand, a spiritual quest without religion becomes a form of stubborn resistance and unwillingness to investigate any further, and a self-assertion stating an almost fearful dependence upon "independence". It becomes a heart without a soul.

Religion without a spiritual quest affirms the mind and ego as being the seat of the soul and denies the heart to its rightful owner. Spirituality alone in a sense affirms the heart, but denies the soul. Acceptance of soul requires the acceptance of religion, at least in general, and the popular abhorrence of religion in general for its authoritarianism and oppression will not allow for that.

So we are caught in the predicament of needing to deny our souls the access to the very purpose of religions, the 'salvation' of the soul.

On Self-expression

Self-expression is the fountain of youth, it is the creator of beauty. It is the hopeless addiction, the frustration of which leads to violence and bloodshed.

Repression is of exactly that - self-expression, whether we are repressing ourselves by taking sides with the oppressor or allowing ourselves to be repressed, as in feeling that being a victim is the necessary route to take to get to our needs.

I discovered the secret of the hopeless addiction to self-expression and realized that nothing could stand in the way of this, and therefore harbored no illusions to the contrary.

When Self is Expressed

When self is expressed, we have a clearly manifested, unburdened soul. When self is ex-pressed, soul is unburdened. Unburdened soul manifests.

The self obscures and burdens the soul, and the soul burdens and confuses the self. The self is also a reflection (mirror/reverse image) of the soul. In much the same way as the soul is created in the image of God.

Self-expression is the unburdening of the soul, which is a manifestation of soul intent. Self-expression in any way is soul-manifestation, the intent of the soul being to unburden itself, to manifest, to emerge.

So we are souls, learning how to express ourselves. And everything, in a sense, is soul manifestation. Or all manifestation is manifestation of soul.

Initial manifestation is with the intention of completion. An initial manifestation is always an intent to complete something.

This is why, in healing, all offers, all manifestations, no matter how 'negatively' perceived, must be accepted, and equally. Because often it is that the perceived positive is as veiling as the perceived negative, but even the veiling is a manifestation of intent to be seen, and must be seen and accepted as such.

Completion is different from initiation. Initiation can take place without completion, but completion cannot occur without initiation.

Without experience, initiation may be fumbling in the beginning, but if allowed to follow its own course of events, the point and final product will be achieved.

This is why it is often said that we must surrender to ourselves - the good, bad and ugly, because we will achieve our goal, if we are not deterred, distracted or discouraged.

Even then, we will, for the most part, figure out some other way. And that's where straightforwardness is lost and things get devious and confusing.

In the absence of security, we will look for a means to create it, because from security, our confidence manifests and it is then OK for us to feel good about ourselves without criticism, and that's the beginning of what we are looking for. In order to feel good, we must feel good about ourselves.

Acting on impulse is the creation of opportunity to challenge validity through the exploration of consequences. It is a search for confidence and a part of the soul intent to have self be all-knowing.

Soul is inviting self to know itself perfectly, as perfect self-knowing is a divine, and therefore soul, quality. Valuable lessons are often learned through trial and error.

It is fortunate if we can learn them in the company of forgiving friends. For this I am thankful for the presence of forgiving friends.

The point and purpose of the religion of Islam (Surrender) is to support and facilitate the clarity of the soul's manifestation. Coming from the truth and leading to the truth, Islam (Surrender) is purifying. Accepting the religion of Islam (even that it exists) is soul purifying.

So True Muslims (Surrendered as the little children are Surrendered) are True faithful Muslims. They are the servants of God Almighty and they Should Start taking responsibility for it.

It is this quality of soul-purification, inherent within Islam, that is observed when it is accepted and practiced with a pure intention. Purity of intention is discovered and manifested more easily when under the guidance of a realized Teacher, for that is the way that True Prophetic Transmission is Received.

In Islam, the truth of one's Surrender to Allah is confirmed at the hand of the Prophet Muhammad, upon whom be Allah's peace and blessings. And, such in the form of a confirmation, or a "permission" to teach. This permission is from Allah and therefore inherently within All of us.

This inherent capacity has also been recognized by the Prophet himself. But its outward confirmation, its proof, activation, fulfillment of potential and maximum effect, is to be found only in the seeking, finding and learning from a TRUE BELIEVER or authorized representative. For how can you have your surrender and self-realization activated, recognized or confirmed by one who is not?

Chapter Eight

The Powers of Bismillah, You and Love

True surrender is more than self-realization, even though self-realization is the beginning, the process and the goal.

Self-realization is the process of healing the mental, emotional and spiritual difficulties inherent in life, and is prerequisite to gratitude and a soulfully motivated willingness to continue by acceptance of further studies.

After self-realization there is self-manifestation, which results from motivation, so there are choices to be made.

Awareness of the field of possibilities and the processes by which choices are made will be expanded and the wisdom must be acquired in the process of learning to make better and more informed choices.

Without self-realization there cannot be love and gratitude, and love and gratitude (either the expression of or quest for) are the only true motivations for accepting Islam (surrender) and walking in the way of the Truth. Fear and obligation will simply not last.

So without healing there cannot be self-realization, and without self-realization there cannot be true responsibility, and without true responsibility there cannot be gratitude, and without gratitude there cannot be love, and without love there is no true motivation.

Until all those truths are realized in one, one is not truly of whole mind and sound body, and is therefore neither required nor able to completely understand and accept the responsibilities of Islam.

So the healing - self-realization - is first. Then we are at least able to join the ranks of the whole men and women of Allah. And willingness (himmah) comes from the soul.

So it is the duty of Muslims (surrendered and enlightened people) to enlighten (lighten the burden of) others, to help them unburden their souls and set themselves free.

It is not, as is often assumed, to burden them by insisting that they share in some form of slavery to religion. A freed people will always come to the aid of their liberators.

ISLAM is the soul purifying power of accepting Surrender. Surrender, and the life in Surrender, is the purpose, manifestation and result of the True Prophetic revelation. ISLAM is the power of Surrender to purify and to cleanse the soul of the dross and residues of mortal life.

In effect, what one is doing when making the prayers, is self-expressing (gratitude), and further cleansing and purifying one's soul by surrendering the heart, body and mind into a divine light, until it becomes so saturated with truth that there is nowhere left for falsehood, the driving illusions, to hide. But this is only for the people who want that.

How can one be truly surrendered and still be all alone? Must it not be realized that there are others gone before and still more to come? It must be realized that surrender and mastery of Truth are a chain, and have a source.

Will a truly surrendered person allow fear of authority to keep her from discovering the loving benefit to be had from a True Servant of God Almighty? I think not.

One may discover the love of Surrender on one's own, and many do. But the understanding of mastery - the permission to manifest it and the ability to transmit it - which is the fully fulfilled and manifested power of self-realization, comes only from having received it by such means.

The remembrance of God, to remember and remind (and lots of it), is the way to manifest. Group and private remembrance practices is the soul manifesting its truth. It is the soul manifesting its desire.

It is the soul manifesting its desire to manifest. It is a manifestation of the desire of the soul to manifest and fulfill its intent. It is a manifestation of the desire of the soul to manifest and fulfill its intent to be fulfilled.

It will be fulfilled. It wills to be fulfilled. It wills to be fulfilled because GOD-REALIZATION wills it to to be fulfilled.

How can Surrender to Allah lead to anything but real fulfillment? How can it be anything but the real fulfillment?

The search for satisfaction or completion (of the mission) is based upon a feeling of emotional dissatisfaction, and not upon Reality. It is to the quest for emotional satisfaction that creation, the composite of the personal worlds of all souls, poses itself as a medium for fulfillment.

Herein lies the distinction between Truth and illusion, but illusion is also truth. Or Reality and illusion, but illusion is also real, and it is in the reality of illusion that the dramas of life are played out. But in Truth, nothing is done.

So it is the emotional body (and the heart is the seat of the emotional body) that is doing the driving. But in Truth there is no emotional body, no driving, and nothing to be done because it is done already by Allah, in Truth!

It is our job to at least believe in this Truth, to recognize it and honor it, and to access it, using it as the true point of reference, as need occurs, and it does, often. And without this Truth, the point of life is lost, and so are souls.

Hence the 'salvation' principle - the idea of 'saving' souls. And Islam (the religion of Surrender) is nothing if not about that.

Our 'world' is here as a place to manifest our soul's intent to know and experience itself fully. And when wasn't that so? Our fulfillment of that intent is in Surrender to it, but our Surrender is not to or for our illusory 'world', but only to and for ALLAH Alone.

He stands alone without any Need for partners, allies, son/s, daughter/s, brother or sister.

The distinction Clear between the Creator and the Created.

Throughout Time Mankind has tried reaching past his capabilities and has tried diminishing ALLAH'S Relevance by adding low human weaknesses such as Jealousy,Anger and vengefullness towards his Creation.

Fearfullness has no logic or place in GOD-REALIZATION.

Only He is! So be He!

Completely emerged

Completely fulfilled

Completely realized

Complete!

"Unhappy people have false beliefs!" ~

Based on earlier determinations we can now posit the peculiar Sense Of Separation carried by most human beings as the primary cause for neurotic behavior (including compulsive normality or conformity), the underlying manifestation of which is a seemingly irremediable insecurity manifesting as an unidentifiable anxiety - an unnerving and unrelenting sense that something is always wrong and needs to be fixed.

We can also posit the misdiagnosis of this unrecognized and untreated potentially minor misconception as a remediable neurosis - and trying to fix it - as the cause of all identifiable major neuroses and psychoses, which manifest as ill health and unpleasant behavior in their search to be healed.

Trying to fix the manifestation necessarily denies its root cause. Trying to fix it posits it as real and therefore potentially remediable. From this false belief come all the so-called remedial attempts that have only served to complicate and obfuscate the real problem, which is a perfectly normal and understandable Sense Of Separation.

All illness and unpleasant behavior is a call for help. This could be recognized as an undeniable truth.

If our primary mission is to know God, and God created us for that, then how can we fail if our will is in sync with Divine Will, and the Divine will be done. (as in finished?)

So if Knowing God is our Primary Mission, and it's done already (need I explain?), why do we not feel complete? Why do we still sense incompleteness? (There are several Islamic traditions about children, heaven and parents that explain this.) Why are we still behaving in response to neurotic behavior patterns? Why are we not at peace - in harmony and joy with ourselves and with others? Why do we still have anxieties which lead to ill health?

Clearing our subconscious predispositions - One theory on the cause of recurring Illness is that recurrence is due to residual subconscious predispositions, to which we naturally revert when our guard is let down or when the "coast seems clear.". Observing and clearing these propensities is an important part of the work.

Perfection is an attitude - a vision, if you will. We can adopt it if we choose. We can choose to see perfection, or we can choose to seek for faults. Fault-finding is actually blame. We're blaming the fault for, and to manifest, our dissatisfaction. In order to blame a fault we have to find one - hence fault-finding.

OR, we can choose to see perfection, and can God see otherwise?

It is only from our Sense Of Separation that we seek. If we had no Sense Of Separation we would not feel the need or desire to SEEK Unity. Why would we seek what is already present?

If we know deep down It Cannot be true and that there is No logic to it, it must be a false belief.

Do not believe just to please others for fear of Persecution, bullying, intimidation or just pure slavery in all it's forms From Mild to very Harsh.

IN my opinion there are Three levels of True Faith linked to One God-REALIZATION.

Level 1 The Realized authentic Faith which has no emotional baggage and devotion is completely To please, seeking to work Right to repair/heal the way back To One God-REALIZATION.

This level of faith may not even be recognised by the owner as anything Special but as the events in one's life unfold recognition of these wonderful qualities of True authentic Humanity will gain True recognition with a Respectfully loving and peaceful existence that will be Truly felt throughout Life.

Level 2 This level of faith is just for yourselves and No one else.

Although One GOD-REALIZATION may be prominent in yourselves the fact that you have limiting intentions on sharing your Good Luck may be your undoing in that you are not fully in sync with the true purpose of creation and the Unity with the One Creator ALLAH Almighty, given different Names by different Languages but with the Same unifying Qualities of True Love,Mercy and compassion.

Level 3 This level of faith is one that is shy to manifest itself.

It may be buried deep within YOURSELVES for a long time too afraid to come out in to YOUR judging World,Wherever you may find yourselves or whatever Label the world has given yourselves.

Never to benefit yourselves Complete or others.

From Emotional blackmail used to keep your Self esteem in control by Fear and threats whether direct or indirect To total Destruction of your Mind,Body and lastly your soul.

The Result is Hell on Earth and Hell in the after life.

Do not be fooled any longer,Slavery comes in different forms.

Free your Mind,Body and your Soul For complete God-REALIZATION.

You can Repair your relationship with Almighty God And instantly do away with this sense of Separation by Following yourselves Complete with Deep Instinct.

Instinct equals Logic in most cases if you rid yourselves of All the Anchored Emotions of others Who in all honesty are less qualified to judge yourselves but Who will sacrifice their souls and damn yourselves forever for The feeling of power.

Wanting this feeling of power if only for a moment over others is Primarily for That brief moment of so called 'High' can be Healed, Substituted or Eradicated with the right Guidance but there has to be a Self-Assertion of this Illness.

If the Sense Of Separation is recognized as the fundamental illusion and the root cause of all dissatisfaction, and all neuroses and psychoses are recognized as extensions and perpetuations of this fundamental illusion, then it would stand to reason that the healing of this Sense of Separation would eliminate the primary fault upon which all neurotic manifestations were constructed.

Throughout historical teachings it seems as though everyone agrees that Unity is the resolution of all problems, and that this Sense Of Separation is the primary agitation that causes acting out and repression.

When we feel One with ourselves everything feels fine. Agitation is an absence of this feeling of Oneness/everything is fine. We then diagnose this agitation and prescribe for it which only distracts us from the cause and posits it as real and somehow fixable.

'Diagnosis and prescription' is the thought form of a mechanic, not of a healer.

Healers look for cause, not changes in the effect.

HEALING THE SENSE OF SEPARATION

If we are NOT separate from God, as that is an impossibility, what is the TRUE Source of the Sense Of Separation which causes the agitation, the desire for the cure of which leads us into all forms of neurotic behavior? What causes us to not simply realize this truth and gain the benefit of it?

THE PRIMARY MISSION THEORY

Understanding our Primary Mission,
the Importance of its Completion
and the Significance of the Absence of its Completion.
If we understand and believe that children are sent by God
to bring Love, Healing & Forgiveness to their parents,
it clarifies the true reasons for illness and methods of healing.

(As children) we won't manifest (our best) as long as there is something else on our minds. And what's always on our minds? At the root of it is the dilemma of the need for self-justification, arising from an unwanted and unconscious compulsion to please our parents or to try to escape from pleasing our parents.

So to that I say this. This attempt to please our parents is the root of all neuroses. It is our search for unconditional love. But even after we've found unconditional love it's hard for us to release our neurosis, our neurotic searching. Putting our neuroses back where they came from is integral to self healing.

Children can never please their parents, it's impossible and they shouldn't have to. Parents must be pleased with their children, which means they must first be pleased with themselves.

If they (the parents) are not (pleased with themselves)(and how many do you know that are?), they look to be pleased and project their need to be pleased onto their children.

In effect, they put their children in the position of needing to please them - which can never be done because they cannot be pleased if they are not already.

If children can negotiate the shift from pleasing their parents to healing them, they can set themselves free and gain the approval they're looking for. And for this they need their parents help.

Illness is caused by a breakdown in communication. As children, we tend to forget what we are scheming for by getting so caught up in the scheme that we believe it ourselves.

So what are we scheming for? Could it be as simple as an innocent expression of love? It appears that in the final analysis, we are left with a simple, unexpressed and probably forgotten desire to communicate our love.

Underneath all our frustration, despair and hopelessness lies an unresolved desire to communicate the well being of our reality to our parents, and ultimately help them to find their own.

The Secret Sister -

Understanding Bulimia

"Yes, I admit that I have a split personality, and kinda insist that everyone does whether they know and admit it or not. Don't we all have "two (or more) sides" to ourselves? Why do we always refer to "a part of me" when we're undecided about something? But in the case of bulimia, I have to admit that there is clearly an insistent side and a persistent side.

"The more "I" insist that I want to be well from it and that it go away, the more "she" persists in hanging around. The more "I" resist, the more "she" persists. "She" seems to accept me pretty well and is patient and ok with my insistence, but "I" do not accept her at all, quite the contrary. I hate and vilify her with my every breath and waking thought. I'm totally obsessed and possessed by her, and want only to be rid of her. So who am I here, really?

"You'd think I'd "get the message" that she's not going to go away, and learn to live with and accept her, but what I think I'd have to go through to do that would be unbearable, I feel so much that I should be ashamed of her.

What's more, I hate and am ashamed of my mom, too, and would rather die than be like her, but I am.

"It seems that my only chance is through understanding, since God knows nothing else (and I've tried literally everything) has worked. So if I'm going to understand this, I'm going to have to discover her secret. And if I'm going to discover her secret, I've got to somehow stop hating her long enough to listen even though I do not like (obviously) what she has to tell me.

"So - if I'm going to listen to her, first I've got to accept her. Hmmmm.

"So who is she, anyway? She's certainly me, but what is she trying to tell me? She's like my secret sister, so "she's" my secret! I know that much, but if she's got a message for me, I've got to get to the state of accepting her before I can hear it.

"But believe me, that's not easy, 'cause it's the one thing I've dedicated my life to not do.

"I'm determined! I will not accept her and I will not accept my mom in her present condition, and I will not accept myself in my present condition - except that myself in my present condition is already a manifestation of my not accepting myself. So I'm certain of only one thing, and that is that I'm really confused. And why not? How could I not be? No one, and I mean absolutely no one, has ever made any sense of, or in, my life.

"So what is this deep secret love that I carry? And what is the secret of this deep secret love that I carry?"

UNDERSTANDING SPIRITUAL HEALING

Spiritual healing is the approach to divinity and divine love is well understood by The people who have made the changes to see the reality as it should be seen.

More recently by the leading edge psychological researchers and groups of western healers looking into all resources to understand reasons and cures for modern diseases.

The most recently discovered foundation to this approach states that the whole of healing is in knowing the difference between conditional and unconditional love, and that it requires support from the people of unconditional love to help the people of conditional love make the transformation.

Evidently, the whole of our self-limiting can be attributed to attempts to meet conditions for love. Yet love is divine, holy and endless and more and more people are coming to that realization daily.

If not, then the first step is getting their attention, getting them to believe and understand it, hence the point of suffering.

It's very clear that until the emotional entanglement around an anchoring issue is cleared, in most cases, attempts to clarify or eradicate that issue will fail. So what are 'anchoring' issues? Anchoring issues are those issues, traumatic or otherwise, that hold a physical incapacity in place.

Conscious Denial and Why People Refuse to Heal.

Our conscious mind is in many stages of denial all at once. We deny remembering everything no matter what and for good reason - even what we ate yesterday. But the entirety of our experience is stored in our memory.

Healing definitely means revisiting - being able to make sense of our lives, rather than exist in a coma of traumatic shock - and people simply do not want to do that.

So rather than heal themselves, they pass their illnesses and the responsibility for healing them on to their children who, understandably begrudged, necessarily shoulder that responsibility.

Eventually, after hostility develops, these children want to cause pain back, they want their parents to show remorse and suffering, to feel something, so they increase the intensity of their illness or behavior. This becomes a vendetta in which one would rather die than forgive and forget.

Even though this may not always be the case, there is still the possibility and it must be taken into consideration just so it will not be overlooked and missed.

Yet among the wise it is known that confession of ignorance is the first step toward gaining wisdom. It's called repentance, or rethinking themselves. It's what we teach our children yet refuse to implement ourselves.

It may be that ALLAH may bless the people who have died through the actions of their descendents who may act as Healing Forces in Changing the lives of those who are Present with themselves In the Time of their lives.

For many people anger and desire for revenge can be so strong that they will rebel against the idea of healing themselves before tasting it.

For many people, sickness is their chosen means of expression for anger, futility, frustration and grief, and of course they do not want to admit that.

So if your sickness is plaguing you and everything you do to help it go away seems to be failing, you might want to look into a well-known trick of the self called PR or Psychological Reversal.

You know if you're doing it! It's quite possible that in spite of all your outward affirmations, you may not really want to get well.

It's possible that your intention has actually degenerated to pure revenge or some other lesser form of drawing attention to the real unspoken problem, rather than to getting well.

If that is the case then your illness is the self-accepted punishment you feel you must suffer for the pleasure you feel in advance for the cruelty you're enjoying afflicting.

It's OK! I understand this and you are not wrong! You feel you've been hurt beyond repair and only getting back looks like any payback at all for the suffering you've endured. But how would it be if I could show you a better way? So you could lighten up on your objects of revenge, and take some of the pressure and the pain off of yourself

The Secret is this - In the perfection of God, there is nothing really wrong, it is only a progression towards understanding that. We need to know what's right, what is really happening underneath our illusions and opinions.

So in God's perfect world, which is present in spite of appearances, everyone is healed (saved) already, but reaching to the understanding.

We help others to reach this understanding by sending them love and healing from our hearts first - by seeing them first in the light of God, as already perfect, healed and progressing toward understanding that.

That sending - of light, love, healing and compassionate understanding - is what heals us! I'm not saying that this is easy to comprehend, but it is the eventuality, if the course of healing is progressing in the right direction.

Healing is what reconnects us with that from which we felt separated. If we are not - never have been and never will be - separated from God, (by virtue of the impossibility) then the question is, where and when did we pick up the feeling or perception of separation?

If there is in reality no separation, what then do we heal? We can only really heal the feeling of separation. And if we are not healing by increasingly feeling our divine connection, then something is getting in the way (often referred to as our 'self' or self-definition).

Most of us feel at least somewhat separated from love or from God. That might even be our primary feeling, and the motivation to feel love would be our primary motivation. But if it's not true that we are or ever have been separated from God or from love, then where did the feeling that we are come from? It came from where we by now no longer want to go or return. The feeling of separation is the result of the perception of rejection by our parents.

On the soul level, that, to us, is completely unacceptable. So according to the theory of our primary mission and in the final analysis, all of our so-called innate hostility can be attributed as a manifestation of our rejection of rejection. And the BIG Question is, "Are we willing to let go of that?"

It's not about getting 'back' to God. We're already there and never weren't. It's about healing our feeling of separation. what is our first experience of that feeling if not our perception of rejection from our parents?

On a soul level, our first spiritual perception of frustration, anger and hostility arises from our perceived inability to connect, to complete our primary mission - that of being a source of love, joy and healing to our parents. We're simply not getting through.

We can only attribute this feeling of separation to rejection. In the infantile framework we have no other point of reference except to connection or rejection. The feeling of rejection can only cause us to get sick and eventually hostile.

We will then spend the rest our lives in an attempt to heal ourselves - our expression of trying to find out and heal "what's wrong" - and discover that it all boils down to our own self imposed reactions to the perception of rejection. Frustration, sickness and hostility all arise from the perception of rejection.

All of our "hostility" is in reality nothing more than a manifestation of our rejection of their rejection. How is it then, not a manifestation of our Love?

As parents learn to heal themselves, their children will respond accordingly!!! Think about that! Think how well it makes you feel to see your parents happy and healed (or does it?). So heal them and teach them this! Don't say it can't be done! It can be done! Here's how, but will you?

HEALING PARENTS

The Primary Mission Theory

Explaining Illness as a Manifestation of Love

First - A Working Hypothesis - What does it mean to have one?

A working hypothesis is a context into which we can place a series of events and from which we can make sense of them, which offers the possibility of an optimistic, positive outcome.

I have found that by accepting this theory and presenting it to others as a working hypothesis, we seem to be able to reach with relative speed and understanding results hitherto unaccomplished in the field of enlightenment and spiritual healing.

In the final analysis, the illness of Bulimia reportedly incurable in a vast majority of sufferers, is not just a cry for help.

It's a social outrage, speaking out in anger, protest and self-suffering against a society that has no mercy for parental anxiety and suffering the whole world over.

It is a cry for understanding, support, healing and forgiveness from these sufferers as children, but not so much for themselves as for their parents. But what we steadfastly refuse to do is take the focus off the kids and put it on the parents! And why is that?

Refusing to Accept Rejection

Looked at from the standpoint of spiritual healing, it will be found that the underlying statement of self-sick children is one of rejection of rejection. The peaceful self-aware soul voice of the sufferer is saying, "I'm really OK in spite of myself and all the things I've taken on to impress you with something.

Don't think I couldn't stop this in a moment if you were ok, but I won't until you figure out why - that it is you that needs help, not me." How do we arrive at this very helpful understanding?

As we all know in one way or another, children are sent from God to be a blessing, a mercy and a healing for their parents. However, they are not always accepted as such. I am proposing that when as babies we are not allowed to perform this divine and holy function it literally makes us sick, which manifest as frustration, confusion and acquired anxiety.

This is currently thought of as the children taking on the anxieties of the parents, and well understood as such, but I am taking it a step further and adding to it a yet deeper dimension by hypothesizing the possibility of an unwavering truth, which I call the Primary Mission Theory, that "Children are sent to bring love and healing to their parents".

It is their primary mission, and that the illnesses they take on are a result of the spiritual frustration coming from an inability to fulfill that mission, coupled with an inability to understand why. So they set out on a quest to understand sickness, and the first they eventually understand, if they succeed, is their own. But it relates directly to the psychological predicament of their parents.

In how many different Times of life does This occur?

It is now proven, if not well known, that Unity heals.

Psychological and emotional investigation shows that releasing emotional blocks increases our capacity to perceive Unity, which in turn brings peace of mind and further enables us to heal and to think well of ourselves.

Since Unity is all that exists, can it not be said that feelings of separation are only feelings, but that it is these feelings themselves that are interfering with our perception of Unity? So if there is no real separation, but only the feelings of separation, where do these feelings come from and how can we prove it and eradicate them?

Experiments have proven to me that even having pleasant thoughts about our parents goes a long way toward increasing our perception of unity and we can actually feel it in the form of an increased feeling of well being.

Reactions to, or varying degrees of acceptance of, the concept of sending love and healing to our parents will quickly show the depth and orientation of the problem.

Spiritual traditions state that children are the secrets of their parents. This is an assertion with profound and mostly unwanted implications.

As the parents of self-sick, angry, violent, neurotic, depressed, destructive, suicidal, bulimic, anorexic, and even murderous children continue to hide their individual versions of dysfunction through the mutually accepted defensive facade of normalcy, these children, forced to accept it, see, feel or suffer the consequences of the fact that their parents do not know how to correctly accept personal responsibility; and in looking outside themselves for some reason for their personal, and in many cases, unrecognized difficulty, they are willing to cast the blame and responsibility on "being born" itself.

That would explain the almost suicidal behaviour of a lot of youngsters when they start to push the boundries of sanity through drugs, drink, sexual experimentation with society disguising or blaming it on Being young hotblooded and irresponsible behaviour of youth.

Fueling the fire that burns inside,Never thinking to quenche it with GOD'S Eternal LOVE.

They soon realize that they have no recourse but to quickly preemptively blame themselves and soon come to believe that there is actually something wrong with them, no matter how hard the parents may, in almost all cases, strive to convince them otherwise.

These children will then, of course, go to great extremes to show and prove "their" (acquired) dysfunction by acting out and creating (almost mocking) manifestations of it.

The false explanation that there is something wrong with the children is gladly accepted by all, and their condition is thereby exacerbated and magnified by being the focus of attention (which is a ruse).

These children, due to their inability or unwillingness to understand and accept that something is wrong with their parents - a difficult realization at best and impossible when you are young, (and which may come somewhat later in life if they are among the lucky ones who find support for this reasoned approach from among their peers) - find that they have no choice but to take on the responsibility, blame and sense of causation for parental dysfunction and therefore must act out the sickness in themselves that they perceive but cannot understand in their parents.

Mind you, it does not have to be and rarely is the same form of illness, but for the purposes of this theory, we'll just say that sickness is sickness, regardless of the manifestation.

This acting out, as it were, in its simplest terms is simply the process of understanding. Naïve and innocent, they literally put themselves on the cross, in the same fire, in order to take on the responsibility of reaching its conclusion.

They take the brunt of the parental illness or disregard and in doing so demonstrate and emphasize their parents' lack of real understanding and self-forgiveness.

Setting aside all reactions, defenses and facades, in every case we will find that there is truth to this hypothesis. Parents must and often do admit to the stark truth of the matter - that they are completely ignorant of what's really going on.

Children are the secrets of their parents. This has been stated in religious and spiritual tradition and the reality of it has been proven and exemplified time and time again.

Societal support for the parental denial involved in the inflicting of children with diagnosable disease adds to the obscuration and mystery of this problem and many children (now become adults) would prefer to, and do, die of (their) dis-ease than give up their family secrets.

Unfortunately, the parents of these children are the witting or unwitting accomplices in this tragedy.

The bottom line is simple and proven if not easy. As parents learn to heal themselves, the children will respond accordingly. Just thinking about it makes one feel better does it not?

The sickness that a bulimic or anorexic child and other less publicised but nevertheless damaging sicknesses that demonstrates This, in its reducible form, is no more than a manifestation of her perception of the sickness in her family.

Her sickness was, and is still, supported by her family and serves its purpose by taking the attention off of themselves, by placing it squarely upon the child.

In her mind and heart, because it is a constructive and purposeful manifestation of her dedication and determination to fulfill her primary mission, it cannot go away (be healed) until her primary mission of bringing love and healing to her parents is accepted.

In order to do that she must heal herself. And in order to do that she must be able to take the blame off herself, which is virtually impossible without this understanding.

Healing Parents - the need for paternal love - its purpose and why we have it

What is the recognizable first and primary motivation of all children, which carries on into life should it not be fulfilled in childhood? It is simply to please - and to please our parents, specifically daddy.

We have to recognize and act upon our need for paternal love because in our minds the reality of it is simply not there. We've simply given up and accepted that we'll never really bring the love and healing to our parents.

For many of us the possibility is no longer even on the horizon. The question in need of healing is - why is it not there? Why are so many, if not all, of us driven by our need or desire for paternal love?

I might go so far as to propose that unconsciously we are driven into the fields of healing and psychotherapy by our need to understand its absence.

We are driven by our desire to heal - but is it just ourselves, and can that ever be enough? I focus here on men because if the men in families are secure and healed, the women and children will more likely be also.

Is not security and the perceived lack of it the major paternal issue? Why do men feel so all alone? Could it be because they are? Have men abandoned each other? Is not security in society the reason for guilds (which means welds or bonds of loyalty and brotherhood)? Is it not the reason for gangs?

How different could it be if gangs were understood in this light and not made wrong and vilified by a society in need of enemies upon whom to wage the war at which they are so experienced and from which they make so much money?

What if it were possible to see that the gangs are simply kids acting out a societal deficiency? Could they not be turned around? Will they be, or will they continue to manifest their insistence upon help for their parents?

Everyone knows that Aikido is the supreme and perfected martial art based on knowing that there is no enemy, only fear, and turning fear, and enemies, into friends. And fear is just the basic survival instinct.

Is it really needed? Or do we, as lonesome, isolated people, only still think that it is? But if we are still operating from that adrenaline rush of having just survived, then even if there is no longer any enemy in sight, we will look to create one out of need to justify our un-calmed war mode.

We are coming out of the lesser battle for survival and into the greater battle of calming and clearing the excited, still fighting self. This is the art of peace - of bringing peace, love and security into ourselves and our world. It's what children, and innocent, secure and unafraid adults, are all about.

With athletes, the warming down is longer in them who took a long time warming up. Whereas athletes who go into battle with a calm heart already established have little or no difficulty returning to it after the event, or even keeping it during.

As parents learn to heal themselves, their children will respond accordingly. Just think about it.

A Passionate Demand for Help

Until Their parents can recognize their part in the creation of these sicknesses, they will not cease to be plagued by them, and the child will not be vindicated and satisfied - released from the self-imposed responsibility to manifest it.

In this case the persistence of the bulimic activity is completely clear of emotional confusion and accepted for exactly what it is, a life saving, self and soul preserving habit acquired as a needed tactic for self preservation. But These habits are hard to kick until they can be heard and understood for what they are - a manifestation and reminder of deep seated resentment, anger and hostility. Then they will simply not be needed any longer.

Clearing the underbrush, the emotional confusion around the acquisition of the habit, requires time and a consistent, properly oriented therapeutic support.

How many self destructive habits have each one of us got that we could offload and find The truth wrapping us up with True Love.

Until the habit itself is deeply understood, it persists in its need to deliver a message. The message is simple, but not easily heard: "Help my parents, not me!"

The illness serves also another function, that of causing the child to investigate herself and the nature and causes of her condition - where it came from, what it is, how and why she took it on, what it is demanding (recognizing its symbolization, what it stands for) - all of which will lead to the inevitable conclusion of hearing a passionate demand for help for her parents.

This line of reasoning does not apply only to this set of symptoms. As we know, we have a whole generation of societies of quietly or actively rebellious children bound and determined to scream on their parents in one way or another, while the parents dutifully seek support in a medically oriented society willing to accept their money in exchange for absolution.

Only the few and the brave among them seek to apply radical techniques of personal responsibility and psycho-spiritual techniques of self investigation to come to proper and satisfying conclusions.

As the evidence to this line of reasoning increases, more and more successful cases will emerge to convince the society at large that radical reform is both necessary and immanent, and it does not involve blame, but necessitates the taking of personal responsibility.

As larger support groups develop even more speedy and radical means towards psychological and emotional clearing, it may pave the way toward a new understanding of the cause and cure of theses illnesses, which will set free a great number of grateful people to increase the universal success of this work.

How to Heal our Parents and Heal Ourseves in the Process

How to Heal Ourselves and Our Parents Too.

(But do we really want to?)

In the meantime, what can we do about it? The gist of this Book points to the necessity of healing parents and taking the focus off of the children instead of intensifying the attempts to treat children as separate from their parents, feeding the misconception that started the problem in the first place.

Given that the parents are unwilling, unavailable or dead, what's a poor child to do? The whole of the frustration and the better part of the healing industry to date is predicated on the hopelessness of this problem. "Get used to it", they say, "adjust".

Adjusting to loss is a huge part of the problem and the focus of much of the industry. And it's all based on recognizing a problem but not knowing what to do, how to heal it.

It is relegated to the realm of the impossible and then we set about the almost impossible task of adjusting (to the impossible). But that's hugely frustrating in its own right, and becomes another part of what seems to be an increasing, endless problem.

All this from the absence of the genuine spiritual Insight that nothing is in reality lost.

No one seems to give any energy to the possibility that it is not impossible. We do not see that doing the work of healing the parents is integral to our own mental and spiritual health.

Doesn't matter whether it 'succeeds' or not, whether we see the 'results' or not (we will, but more on that later). What matters is that we cannot truly heal without doing the work, regardless of manifest outcome, it is integral to our health to bring love and healing to our parents - to OUR health .

Since we do not see that, we simply give up on the project and surrender to the adjustment process that is so prevalent in psychotherapy today.

It is Possible! And as stated before, not only possible but necessary. And we WILL see results, and most immediately in ourselves and in our parents, and it does not at all matter whether they are "alive" or "dead".As a final Note of Peace :May I wish All my Readers Wonderful joyous lives.May you find ALLAH'S LOVE all around you Forever.

All my Love and Peace

JAVED